DATE DUE

What would Steve Jobs do?

What would Steve Jobs do?

How the Steve Jobs Way Can Inspire
Anyone to Think Differently and Win

PETER SANDER

New York Chicago San Francisco Lisbon
London Madrid Mexico City
Milan New Delhi San Juan Seoul
Singapore Sydney Toronto

The *McGraw·Hill* Companies

1 2 3 4 5 6 7 8 9 10   DOC/DOC   1 6 5 4 3 2 1

ISBN 978-0-07-179274-5
MHID 0-07-179274-0

e-ISBN 978-0-07-179275-2
e-MHID 0-07-179275-9

McGraw-Hill books are available at special quantity discounts
to use as premiums and sales promotions or for use in corporate
training programs. To contact a representative, please e-mail us
at bulksales@mcgraw-hill.com.

This book is printed on acid-free paper.

CONTENTS

INTRODUCTION

Steve's brilliance, passion and energy
were the source of countless innovations
that enrich and improve all of our lives.
The world is immeasurably better because
of Steve.

—Apple Inc. company statement,
October 5, 2011

"Stay hungry, stay foolish."

That's what Steve Jobs told us all on June 12, 2005, when he gave the now-famous 2005 commencement address to the graduating students of Stanford University.

In that address, he told three stories: about "connecting the dots," about love and loss, and about death. It was a moving speech. It moved everybody in the audience. It moved many of us beyond that Stanford audience, the many fans of Jobs who had heard of his cancer diagnosis a year earlier.

It has moved a lot of people since then.

Among all commencement addresses, Steve's 2005 address is the clear winner, as measured by YouTube viewings. On September 10, 2011, Steve Jobs led this race by a comfortable margin. The 2005 speech had been viewed 5,268,012 times. The runners-up were Carnegie Mellon's dying professor-turned-writer Randy Pausch with 1,371,075 views, Will Ferrell's 1,176,606 views for Harvard 2003, and Oprah's 716,982 views for her 2008 address to a similar Stanford audience.

We were all following Steve's lead and his sage advice even then. But by October 10, 2011, that same Stanford address had been viewed 11,022,670 times. That's a gain of roughly six million views in the five days after he passed away on October 5, 2011.

I can think of no better way to measure the adoration of Steve's followers, who hail from so many parts of the human race. What other business leader would have come close? What other business leader has garnered the attention of so many in the business world, so many in the academic world, and so many in the consumer world? How many, beyond the 40,000 employees inside of Apple, consider him one of the great guiding lights and leaders of the free world?

I saw the flowers. I saw the apples. I personally saw the pictures and letters and everything else that made up the memorial left in front of Apple's Cupertino headquarters on One Infinite Loop. By the Saturday following Steve's passing, those memorials would have covered a tennis court. The memorials left in front of 357 Apple Stores around the world were equally moving, if not as large in size.

How did he gain this status? How did he become a guru? How did he get the nod as the world's greatest technology leader, and one of the greatest leaders, period, of all time? How did Steve "beat out" Microsoft's Bill Gates, who consistently captured more than 80 percent of the personal computing market and had more than five times the wealth Steve did? How many of us, even those who don't own Apple products, revere the man for what he did and wish we could mimic even a piece of his innovative genius and leadership formula?

How many of us, especially in the business world, wish we could rise to the plateau of name-brand status? And not just name brand, but our *first* name as the brand—"Steve"? Not Michael Jordan, but just plain "Mike." Just like Mike. Be like Mike. Not Steve Jobs, but just Steve. Steve, a true superstar.

President Barack Obama may have summed it up as well as anyone: "The world has lost a visionary. And there may be no greater tribute to Steve's success than the fact that much of the world learned of his passing on a device that he invented."

$380 BILLION

Leaders can be adored and admired for a wide range of reasons, from a gripping personality and humor all the way to saving the Union. Business leaders are admired for creating successful businesses. On that note, the legacy of Apple Inc. speaks for itself: $380 billion. Billion with a "B." That's how much the financial world, aka the stock market, values Apple Inc.

That's just a number, right? It may not seem like a lot in today's world of trillion-plus-dollar budget deficits, $700 billion "TARP" programs, and such. But for a company, it's huge.

It makes Apple the largest publicly traded manufacturing corporation in the world. And, while Apple and oil giant ExxonMobil vie for the honor of being the world's largest company period, the Apple story is far more compelling. Why? Because Apple produces a *product*—a product that it must sell in a competitive marketplace.

Apple must sell a product that absolutely no one needs, that must be wanted or desired and must be better than the competition's if the cash register is to ring.

Can we say the same about oil and petroleum products? No way. In fact, the next five companies by market cap produce oil, mine metals, or move money around—but don't produce anything so intricate or that must pass customer judgment the way an Apple product must.

In fact, moving down the list to number 7, Microsoft, the next company that really makes anything, one wonders whether it meets the same standard as Apple. It seems that few people really *want* Microsoft products, but like oil and its refined products, they must buy and use them. They have no choice: like oil products, they get you where you're going; they're an industry standard.

The Apple racehorse passed the Microsoft plow horse at $222 billion in market cap in May 2010. You can see how fast that horse is running, for in late 2011 Apple is at $380 billion, while its longtime rival is stuck at $228 billion. At the time Apple passed Microsoft, Exxon was still number 1 at $279 billion, but it has since managed to hold the place position at $358 billion.

That's pretty amazing. But the finish, in first place or otherwise, isn't really the point. What really makes the Apple story so amazing is not just its exceptional products and financial success but the context in which the company has arisen.

Consider that Apple is a mere 35 years old. Although Microsoft too rose quickly through the ranks, how many companies have risen so far and so fast? With no mergers and virtually no acquisitions? None. If you consider that Apple's valuation was somewhere around $3 billion in 1997 when Steve Jobs returned to the helm, and $10 billion in 2003 before the iPod really took off, Apple, under Steve's leadership, has unquestionably created more value more quickly than any other company in history.

The evidence is indisputable. Although, as we'll see, Steve Jobs was far from a "textbook" business leader, we know what he brought to Apple in terms of customer savvy, vision, product knowledge, and marketing genius. We'll share that in this book. We also know what happened when Apple was in the hands of other individuals, which it was more than once during its brief history. It wasn't pretty.

ANATOMY OF A SUPERSTAR

Innovation consultant Nicholas Webb, in his book *The Innovation Playbook* (Wiley, 2010), offers a list of traits, taken largely from the sports world, that define a *superstar*:

- Superstars are consistently better than the rest.
- You can count on superstars to deliver.
- Superstars are role models; you want to be like them.
- Superstars are good in all aspects of the game, not just one part of it.
- Superstars (usually) have a balanced and accessible personality to go with their talent.
- Superstars are team players, and they make everyone else better.
- If superstars were a culture, you'd be comfortable being part of that culture.

Now, against this standard, Steve does pretty well, right? Indeed, it's hard not to look at him as the Michael Jordan or Wayne Gretzky or Willie Mays or Martin Luther King of the business and technology world.

It's a world that hasn't produced many superstars, certainly not with the worldwide recognition of Steve. Certainly not deserving of flowered, appled memorials.

THE CORE IDEA

We can worship at the altar of Apple, and we can worship Steve Jobs all we want. But I want to be clear about the purpose of this book.

- *What Would Steve Jobs Do?* is not a biography of Steve Jobs.
- *What Would Steve Jobs Do?* is not a history of Apple Inc.

Biographies of Steve and histories of Apple have already been done, and done well. There's no need for another "me too" book on the business shelf. Several titles can already be found that focus on innovation, how Apple does innovation, and how Steve Jobs supported and led innovation.

The point of *What Would Steve Jobs Do?* is not just to recall or recount the successes of Apple and Steve Jobs. It is to capture the essence of what Steve Jobs has done as a *leader*. It's about what *you* can take away from Steve's style and success and apply to *your* organization. Sure, much of Steve's success was based on innovation, and creating an innovation culture is a major component of his leadership success.

We, as leaders, have a responsibility to manage innovation in our organizations. An organization that doesn't innovate is dead in the water, ready to be sunk by the progress of technology, the competition, or both. An organization that doesn't innovate is not responding to its customers, nor is it responding to the outside world.

No doubt, Steve did innovation well. But there was something else, something above and beyond, that got millions to follow him—millions inside and outside his organization. There was something that got us to tune in to that Stanford address, to leave flowers in front of the local Apple Store, and to pause and reflect on the day he died. There is something above and beyond the "Thomas Edison meets Willy Wonka" image that is occasionally used to describe Steve.

Steve Jobs proved himself to be both a titan of American business and a titan of our personal experience. Nobody else in history has come close to achieving that status.

The world is immeasurably better for his existence. *What Would Steve Jobs Do?* attempts to capture how he did it.

A ROAD MAP TO EXCELLENCE

What Would Steve Jobs Do? has two parts. The first three chapters give some context, a "core" (sorry about that) of Apple's history blended with Steve's own personal bio as a foundation for understanding his leadership style. We then examine today's conventional views of leadership and appraise how Steve was different, arriving at the six-part Steve Jobs Leadership Model.

The remaining six chapters cover the six parts of that model: Customer, Vision, Culture, Product, Message, and Brand. As much as possible, I lay out each critical piece in Steve's uniquely "elegant, simple" style, capturing what you can do to "think different" about your business and your organization.

Read on, stay hungry, and stay foolish.

CHAPTER 1

BORN

What a computer is to me is the most remarkable tool that we have ever come up with. It's the equivalent of a bicycle for our minds.

—*Steve Jobs, 1991*

Without doubt, the whole Apple story began with the birth and growth of Steve Jobs, whose birth preceded the birth of Apple Computer by just 21 years. His early years were formative and revealing, and are definitely a big part of the Apple story and the development of Steve's leadership style.

Apple's early years obviously represented a very creative and entrepreneurial phase in Steve's life and career. His salesmanship was vital to getting the new product off the ground. His counterculture vision helped the entire enterprise steer clear of the prevailing wisdom of the day: that computers were things that belonged in the data center and were handled only by professionals. Steve saw beyond the status quo, recognized what computers could do, especially if they were combined with the right software, and knew how to sell the idea to the public.

What Steve was leading in this era was essentially a garage enterprise, but he also showed his mettle at managing large groups to produce technical and product accomplishments. While he seemed to know that he needed experienced business leaders alongside of him ("adult supervision"), he didn't necessarily share their views.

He grew suspicious of corporate-style thinking and bureaucracy, and eventually left Apple in a feud with then-CEO John Sculley and the board of directors, even though many of the directors had been picked by Steve himself. But did that end Steve's career as an innovator, entrepreneur, and leader? Hardly. It led to an amazingly successful "rebirth" 10 years later (which will be covered in Chapter 2).

EARLY ADOPTION

Steve Jobs's entry into the world was anything but mainstream from the start. He was born in San Francisco on February 24, 1955, to a pair of unwed 23-year-old University of Wisconsin graduate students. His father, a native Syrian named Abdulfattah "John" Jondali, went on to become a political science professor, while his mother, then Joanne Simpson, became a speech language pathologist. Although the couple would later marry—and produce the novelist Mona Simpson as a biological sister—they placed their first and then unborn son up for adoption.

Adopted he was, by Paul and Clara Jobs of Mountain View, California, an emerging suburban community about 45 miles south of San Francisco, 10 miles south of Stanford University, and at the edge of what would eventually become the heart of Silicon Valley.

Now, Steve's biological parents had one condition for the adoptive parents: that they be college graduates. It's unclear why this condition was ignored, but neither of his adoptive parents had finished college; in fact, his adoptive father had never graduated from high school. But they did pledge their life savings to send Steve to college. They were loving parents and supported everything the curious and energetic Steve wanted to do.

And yes, Steve did go to college—to Reed College, an intellectually charged private liberal arts college in the forested southern inner suburbs of Portland, Oregon. He went for one semester, then dropped out.

But before that, Jobs had attended the mainstream local schools, Cupertino High School and Homestead High School, both less than two miles from what is now Apple headquarters. In the early 1970s, the South Bay Area was changing rapidly from fruit orchards to attractive and clean new suburbs with beautiful streetscapes, plenty of trees, and earth-toned homes for everyone.

Not everything was modern; the local landmark Moffett Field had (and still has) two large hangars that were originally built for dirigibles. The major street corner closest to where Apple's headquarters is today featured a huge prune processing plant. But for the most part, there was a newness and excitement about the area, close to Stanford University, where some of the original research and development that led first to the transistor, then to the semiconductor and printed-circuit board took place. The high-tech boom was beginning.

Steve enjoyed the South Bay Area weather and "vibe" just as any teen would. But he also developed a fascination with electronics. Before he reached his teen years, he attended a demonstration of computers (really just terminals) at the NASA Ames Research Center, co-located at Moffett Field (the site of the dirigible hangars). From that point on, Steve really thrived on being around the many engineers and professionals in the high-tech business.

While in high school, curious Steve attended after-school lectures at the Hewlett-Packard Company in nearby Palo Alto (the home of Stanford). In 1970, a mutual friend introduced him to his early partner and tech whiz, Steve Wozniak (known as Woz), who was five years his senior. Woz, who had also gone to Homestead High School, was in college, but also worked at HP. In the summer of 1972, Steve Jobs worked as a summer employee alongside Steve Wozniak.

Steve Wozniak was working as a technician on what would eventually become a minicomputer. Steve Jobs wondered whether a computer on a single printed-circuit board could be made and sold.

OPEN CIRCUIT

But that idea took a long time to bear fruit. Steve graduated from high school and headed off to Reed for that fall semester in 1972. But Steve was a creative guy back then, and he had already adopted his long-serving motto, "Do what you love to do." College structure really wasn't something that Steve loved. He started exploring other possibilities. He wanted something that he could get passionate about.

At that point in his life, he had no idea what that something really was. But it was pretty clear even then that it wasn't going to fit the mainstream path that most people in that era aspired to: go to college, get a degree, take a job, and rise through the ranks. Steve was different.

Instead, Steve hung on in the Reed area and hung out with friends, reportedly raising cash by collecting soda bottles and getting some free meals at the local Hare Krishna temple. He audited a few classes he was interested in. He was what most people at the time would have called a hippie.

Most famously, he audited a calligraphy class. That class piqued his interest in graphic design, especially in the beauty, appeal, and proportion of different type fonts. It was an epiphany in disguise, for later Steve would draw on that experience to define the Macintosh as a graphics-based machine. "If I had never dropped in on that course, the Mac would have never have had multiple typefaces or proportionally spaced fonts," he shared years later.

ENLIGHTENMENT

By 1974, Jobs had been exposed to a lot of new things, among them the spiritual life and culture of India. He

returned to the Bay Area and, circling back to his interest in electronics, took a job at video game maker Atari,
then a booming Valley outfit. His goal: to earn enough
money for a trip to India, a spiritual retreat.

Never one to stop short of a goal, Steve traveled to
India. He traveled with Reed College buddy Daniel
Kottke, who eventually became the first employee at
Apple. The purpose of the trip was to gain spiritual
enlightenment from the popular Hindu guru Neem
Karoli Baba, but he had passed away before Steve and
Daniel managed to get there. It's not completely clear
what Steve and Daniel did in India, but they came back
Buddhists with shaved heads and traditional Indian
clothing.

One thing that *is* clear is that they experimented with
psychedelics, notably LSD. Perhaps we really don't want
to know more, but Steve did call these experiences "one
of the two or three most important things [he] had done
in [his] life." They certainly triggered his creative juices,
and would be a natural cradle for the "think different"
mantra he carried through life and used for years as a
tagline for Apple products.

Then it was back to America, back to Atari, and back
to hanging out alongside his old buddy Steve Wozniak.
Many people speculate that if Jobs hadn't met Woz
before his trip to India, he would have been leading yoga
chants in some far-off land for the rest of his life.

THE APPLE I, ALMOST A COMPUTER

Woz was what we would now call a nerd, an electronics and computer geek second to none (they probably called him something like that then, too). He became a whiz at circuit-board design and was still with Hewlett-Packard while attending classes at the University of California at Berkeley. He helped Jobs win a challenge at Atari to reduce the number of chips on a circuit board.

Woz had gotten Jobs interested in the Homebrew Computer Club, a local group of computer hobbyists and hackers that met regularly, before the India trip. After Jobs returned, he pressed Woz further on the idea of developing a single-board computer.

He wanted to develop such a computer just to see if they could, and to show it off and sell it to Homebrew members. But he was also thinking bigger. He wanted to start a company. According to Wozniak's account, Jobs told him that "even if they weren't successful, they could at least say to their grandkids they had their own company."

They pooled their resources. Jobs sold a Volkswagen van, and Woz sold an HP calculator, among other things, to raise $1,300, which they used for the materials they needed to assemble some prototypes. Although many liken the story to Hewlett and Packard's 1939 garage beginnings, this project started in Jobs's bedroom and eventually moved to the garage.

By all measures, this was a primitive machine. It was what we would today call a motherboard, with a CPU, memory, and textual video chips. There wasn't much memory, though—4 kilobytes, compared to today's machines with 4 gigabytes, or a million times the memory. There was no keyboard, monitor, power supply, or case. The user had to supply these items. Software was the BASIC programming language; the monitor was typically an old TV. Really, it was an electronics kit along the lines of those sold by Heathkit or Radio Shack, a popular activity in those days.

The so-called Apple I went on sale in July 1976 for $666, with a production cost of $500. That sale price would be about $2,600 in today's terms. A Mountain View computer shop known as The Byte Shop sold completely built-up versions of the Apple I.

EXECUTEK? OR APPLE COMPUTER?

And where did the name "Apple" come from? Along with calligraphy, it was another of the epiphanies from Steve's Oregon years. While in Portland, he got connected with a Zen-influenced (naturally) commune called the All-One Farm.

Steve returned to the farm periodically to work and hang out. And, of course, the All-One Farm grew apples. He admired apples for their simple, appealing look. Later, when Woz picked Steve up at the airport after one of those trips, they talked about the new computer project, which was then still in the works. Steve simply blurted out, "I've got a great name—how about 'Apple'? Apple Computer?"

Many people also attribute the name to Jobs's well-known love for music, and the Beatles in particular, and others attribute it to images of Isaac Newton and great ideas falling out of an apple tree. Those references probably played a part, but the real story is that although they spent hours thinking of other geekier names like "Matrix Computer" and "Executek," none of them really worked—so the name "Apple" stuck.

The whole sequence was a great example of how Woz's technical ingenuity mixed with Jobs's vision and marketing ingenuity. They sold about 200 Apple Is, started designing Apple IIs, and the rest is history.

Rejection? So What: The Vision Gains Momentum

The Apple II story is where the Apple Inc. that we know today really got going. Before venturing into that story, however, it's worth noting that Woz, newly married and with a decent-paying job at HP, wasn't quite sold on the idea of becoming an entrepreneur, so he pitched the idea of developing a microcomputer to the powers that be at HP. As we all now know, that went nowhere.

Still, Steve Jobs had big ideas and a grand vision for their microcomputer. He felt strongly that computers could be something other than large, impersonal, ugly gray machines that sat in a data center and could be touched only by programmers. He visualized "freedom from an IBM-controlled universe" for millions, while IBM and others, like HP, dismissed the Apple-style machine as being "too small to do serious computing." Although his visions didn't crystallize until the introduction of the Macintosh eight years later, in 1984, they were definitely on Jobs's mind back in the mid-1970s.

Jobs quite clearly felt that the lives of individual people (consumers at home; engineers, scientists, and businesspeople in the workplace; teachers at school—you name it) could be improved with the use of a computer. But as the world was eventually to find out, the vision wasn't about the computer; it was about what the computer could do.

The mold for the visionary leadership and boundless passion of Steve Jobs had been cast.

FROM GENESIS TO EXODUS

While the Apple I represents the genesis of the product and the idea of personal computing, the real genesis of the business came with the development and sale of the Apple II. That came in early 1977. This section covers

Steve and Apple from that point through his exodus—his first departure from the company, which came shortly after the 1984 launch of the revolutionary Macintosh.

As we will see, Steve's leadership style really started to take shape during this period, but it came into conflict with the more traditional approaches employed by the bureaucracy that had started to build up around him. Naturally, Steve didn't let the masses deter him; in fact, as we will also see, Steve Jobs's exodus from Apple may have been the best thing that ever happened to him.

The Vision Expands: Apple II

Steve and Woz incorporated Apple on January 3, 1977. Prior to that incorporation, they had brought in a third partner, an older and more experienced Atari draftsman named Ronald Wayne, to help out and to "break ties" when the two Steves couldn't agree on something. When they incorporated, they bought Wayne out for a reported sum of $800 (a stake that would be worth tens of billions today).

The vision of personal computing continued to grow. The Apple II was a complete product, with a case and a power supply and a keyboard; it looked like a computer. It supported color and sound and had eight expansion slots, and shortly after its introduction, it came with a

5¼-inch floppy drive. Now users could easily store and retrieve data—and share that data with other machines. As with the Apple I, Woz was the technical genius behind it, while Jobs provided the vision, the inspiration, and the marketing genius in front of it.

The few thousands that Jobs and Wozniak had invested in the business quickly proved not to be enough. They needed a partner. They needed a little adult supervision as well, because now they were entering the business world in a big way. And neither of them had much experience or know-how with that new can of worms.

MIKE MARKKULA

In 1977, Jobs visited a couple of prominent venture capitalists. Some of them were intrigued and referred him to others, but at least one of them reacted to Jobs's hippie appearance and shied away with, "Why did you send me this renegade from the human race?" Jobs didn't "get the girl" with that interview, but he was introduced to a veteran and semiretired Intel engineer named Mike Markkula. Markkula liked the story and its presenter, and committed $250,000 to the cause in return for a one-third ownership.

Markkula was to play a key business leadership role, mostly in the background and in support of what Jobs and Woz were doing in those early days. He eventually became chairman from 1985 through 1997. He was all business, though, and, ironically, he sided with the team that eventually forced Jobs out in 1985. Still, in those early years, Markkula provided a solid business base for Jobs's vision and operations. Jobs recognized and made good use of Markkula's business skills, just as he recognized and made good use of Woz's technical skills.

Good leaders realize what they don't do well, and develop strong right-hand man relationships with others to get things done.

A KILLER APP

As often happens in the computer industry, the challenge became software. People were fascinated with the product, which was often sold in department stores like Macy's, but the typical Macy's shopper was far from ready or willing to write programs in BASIC. What was needed was what today would be called a "killer app," and indeed one came along, but not until 1979: Software Arts's VisiCalc.

VisiCalc, which was similar to today's Microsoft Excel spreadsheet program, really made it possible for users to do great things with their computers. They could do personal work and work in the workplace, and they could use the 5¼-inch floppy to bring their work home with them and vice versa. It opened up a whole new market for personal computing, reaching far beyond the hobbyists and aficionados.

A Trip to the PARC

The Apple II rolled along, generating annual sales of some $300 million and making Jobs and Wozniak almost instant multimillionaires. But of course, the story doesn't end there.

They got the opportunity to bring a team of engineers to Xerox's Palo Alto Research Center, a cradle for ideas that, unfortunately for Xerox, didn't turn into Xerox products. Jobs got PARC to grant his engineers three days of access and observation in return for 100,000 pre-IPO Apple shares (again, worth billions today). PARC had numerous ideas under development, including what would become laser printing technology and, most important for this story, the GUI, or graphical user interface, which today is more widely known as the computer mouse.

To their credit, the PARC scientists were a bit leery of letting Apple in on their secrets. As a testimonial to having the right versus the wrong vision at the top levels, one PARC scientist quipped: "After an hour looking at demos, they [Apple] understood our technology and what it meant more than any Xerox executive understood it after years of showing it to them." (That scientist, Larry Tesler, eventually joined Apple.) Jobs called the group a "bunch of copier heads" who had "no clue about what a computer could do."

Jobs clearly saw what lay ahead: "a computer for the rest of us."

A MAC IN EVERY HOUSEHOLD

Jobs and his team returned from PARC with the inspiration to add the GUI to a feature-rich machine that was under development, known as the Lisa. The Lisa brought GUI to the forefront and was intended to make Apple a serious player in the business world, but it was not a commercial success because of its high price tag ($10,000).

Mike Markkula had recruited a new CEO, Mike Scott, to run things. Jobs was still chairman, and he was a visionary leader, to be sure, but he wasn't CEO. He was never given the CEO job; others (and possibly Steve himself) preferred to bring in Markkula and Scott, and others later on, to handle this task and provide the necessary adult supervision mentioned earlier. Meanwhile, in 1979, a technical writer and publications expert hired by Apple by the name of Jef Raskin sold the company on a vision of a smaller, fully integrated machine that would be capable of doing what eventually became desktop publishing. By 1979, Markkula and Jobs were sold on the project and asked Raskin to lead the way.

The Macintosh project, reportedly named after Raskin's favorite kind of apple, McIntosh (but spelled differently because of trademark concerns with a high-end audio manufacturer by that name), was kicked off.

The Mac project was much more aligned with both Steve's vision and his personality. He saw it as a way to bring computing to the common man, and he was skeptical of the efforts by the Lisa team (and the developers of the Apple III, which had a very short life because of technical problems) to lure the business community. Steve became the de facto leader of the Mac team.

Meanwhile, Jobs and others had become disillusioned with Scott and started a search for a new CEO. Among other things, Steve wanted someone with a stronger consumer focus and a consumer marketing background. That led, at the recommendation of two recent Stanford hires, to the then-CEO of PepsiCo, John Sculley.

Sculley refused at first, feeling uncomfortable about going to a relatively new and less stable company and being inexperienced with technology. Jobs convinced him with the now-famous line: "Do you want to spend the rest of your life selling sugared water, or do you want a chance to change the world?"

Sculley joined the team, and at first he and Jobs got along famously. Sculley managed the enterprise, the "go-to-market maze," and put the external face on Apple, the company. Steve brought the Mac project to life. The two managed together and went to meetings together; they were "joined at the hip."

At the time, Apple had about 4,000 employees— 3,000 of them working on the Apple II, and, of the remaining 1,000, about 900 working on Lisa and 100 working on Macintosh. The Mac team worked more or less like a start-up, with 80- to 90-hour weeks not being uncommon, while the rest of the company had become quite corporate in nature.

Steve's involvement was deep and wide, and he sweated every detail. When a software glitch was found, he would not let the product ship with downsized software labeled "demo." He was a perfectionist, and he held the team to that standard.

The Mac was a unitized machine, meaning that it was sold as a complete package with no add-ons. It was simple, and it was smaller than anything on the market. It used Sony's new 3.5-inch floppy drive. Unlike any computer before it, it was fully graphical and GUI-driven, with icons and pull-down menus, and with a mouse as its main controlling device. It was, like Steve himself, consumer-friendly, visionary, and somewhat countercultural for the time.

The Ad

The Mac was ready for launch in 1984. It was a big product, and Apple wanted to communicate a big vision, delivered in a big ad, for the big game—the 1984 Super Bowl. The IBM PC had been introduced a couple of years earlier and had gained traction with users and developers, especially in the business space, and, well, IBM was IBM. So Apple's long-time ad agency Chiat/Day came up with a radical antidote. The theme was taken from George Orwell's *1984*, and the ad featured dronelike workers staring at a screen, which was eventually shattered by an energetic young woman to a voiceover: "On January 24, Apple Computer will introduce Macintosh. And you'll see why 1984 won't be like *1984*."

Sculley was uncomfortable with the ad. The board of directors hated it. Steve Jobs, of course, loved it. Steve Wozniak said, "This ad is us." The marketing VP, faced with running a less inspiring ad, decided to run it.

Today, the ad is considered a masterpiece and one of the most effective advertising efforts of all time. But it illuminated the differences between Steve, Mike Sculley, and the rest of the company's leadership.

First Departure

Mac sales were good at first, but then sagged because of a flagging economy and the exhaustion of the early-adopter crowd. At $2,000, the Mac was still expensive, and there wasn't that much software to run on it. That changed in 1985, with the introduction of the Laser-Writer and the Aldus PageMaker software package.

The LaserWriter, one of the first commercially successful laser printers, was part of Jobs's grander vision to make the Macintosh, and computers in general, "do useful things." Not only did it create the new desktop publishing market that Raskin had conceived in the first place, but its visual and graphic strengths established Apple at the forefront for creative and graphics types for years to come.

But still all was not well with the company, given the differences in vision and style between Jobs and Sculley and others, who were seeking a more mature business model. Jobs and Sculley could not agree on how to market the Mac. Sculley wanted to market it to businesses and hired a large sales force to do just that. He wanted to control shelf space at distributors, mimicking the soft-drink distribution model. Jobs saw the Mac as a consumer product, and wanted to set up direct distribution from FedEx facilities to speed service, reduce distribution channel investment, and provide better customer touch—a precursor to the successful Dell direct business model.

Jobs and Sculley couldn't agree on this or a lot of other things. The company was becoming more organization- and sales channel–driven, and less product-driven. It drove Steve nuts, and, unfortunately, many company notables, including Mike Markkula, sided against him. Sculley told Steve that the Mac group was no longer his to run; he would be sidelined to chief technology officer. Wanting no part of this, what did Steve do? He got in his car and drove off—for what would turn out to be 11 years.

In later testimony for the 1995 Smithsonian Awards Program oral history, Steve discussed the problem—which wasn't the company's rapid growth or the side-tracking of his career, but a fundamental shift in values from a product-driven organization to a money-driven one. Steve, quite correctly, saw money as an effect and product as the cause—if you stayed focused on the product, the cash registers would ring. The management team was applying too much MBA stuff (standard business practices), taking the focus off the product and diluting the vision. It wouldn't work for a product-driven company that thrived on innovation.

In a scathing comment during that same interview, Jobs claimed, "John Sculley ruined Apple, and he ruined it by bringing a set of values to the top of Apple which were corrupt and corrupted some of the top people who were there, drove out some of the ones who were not corruptible, and brought in more corrupt ones and paid themselves collectively tens of millions of dollars and cared more about their own glory and wealth than they did about what built Apple in the first place—which was making great computers for people to use."

Sculley, for his side of the matter, wrote in his memoir *Odyssey* that Jobs "was a zealot; his vision so pure that he couldn't accommodate that vision to the imperfections of the world." He went on to discredit Jobs's vision as a "lunatic plan," as "high tech could not be designed and sold as a consumer product."

Sculley and Jobs were clearly like oil and water, although they may have given some balance to each other for a while. It was definitely a learning experience for Steve, and it probably strengthened his resolve to take a different path, for instance, in setting up his own retail store channel instead of vying for shelf space in the existing channels.

Despite their differences, Sculley and Jobs eventually began to recognize each other's contributions to Apple's legacy. They occasionally exchanged e-mails. When Jobs resigned, Sculley sent a note: "Steve, I owe you a lot. Because you cared so much, the universe is a little bit different. You did it with taste, design, addictive user experience, and no compromise products that make us all smile. . . . John."

John Sculley and the rest of the world may not have felt this way when Jobs left in 1985. But after gaining two more business experiences and returning to Apple in 1996, Jobs started down a path that would make Sculley's sentiment speak for most of us.

CHAPTER 2

BORN AGAIN

I think if you do something and it turns out pretty good, then you should go do something else wonderful, not dwell on it for too long. Just figure out what's next.

—*Steve Jobs*, NBC Nightly News, *2006*

According to most accounts, Steve initially didn't handle his departure from Apple very well. But, as we'll soon see, it was a maturing experience. Never one to give up, Steve soon started another company, NeXT Computer, sort of a high-end Apple, with the idea of producing a sort of high-end Macintosh. He used a considerable amount of his own personal fortune to launch NeXT, which largely turned out to be a flop. He also got the chance to buy the computer animation and graphics arm of Lucasfilm, which became Pixar. But instead of selling expensive graphics workstations, it serendipitously morphed into a full-length feature film producer through a surprise arrangement with Disney.

With both companies, but especially with Pixar and Disney, Steve got a chance to work with the big boys and to match his creative energies with some powerful business and market forces. In the case of NeXT, he mostly failed, but he took away some good experiences and learned a lot about interconnectivity, software, and other building blocks that would ultimately shape the next generation of Apple products. At Pixar, he learned a lot about managing large technical teams in a creative environment, and about "big business" dealings from working with Disney.

When Steve made his "Cinderella" return to Apple in 1996, he found a total mess. The company was losing money and had largely resigned itself to occupying a very specialized and slowly shrinking market niche. He was now prepared to almost single-handedly transform the company from a backwater computer maker to the digital powerhouse we now know today. Most observers don't think this would have happened without Steve's 11-year hiatus. Steve would have agreed.

In these years, his leadership style carried forward with its intense customer sense, vision, and product sense, but also added a degree of maturity needed to work in a large corporate environment. He also developed a stage presence and a product face that hasn't been matched in the history of business.

WHAT CAME NEXT

Although he was worth $200 million at the time, Steve Jobs wasn't about to stop creating products or chasing his vision after he left Apple. What would Steve do? Easy— he'd start another company.

He started the appropriately named NeXT Computer, Inc., with a lot of his own money. The goal was to design the "next-generation Macintosh," a more powerful dream machine targeted toward high-powered end users and the higher education market. While NeXT did become the first true Internet Web server, it was too expensive and too fancy, with not enough software to really succeed, but the core operating system developed for it became the model for the highly successful OS X ("OS Ten") operating system. The OS elements became the main ticket for Steve's late 1996 return to Apple and brought success back to the company.

NeXT also gave us another breakthrough in the form of NeXTMail, an early manifestation of Steve's vision that computers should be interpersonal, that is, networked. NeXTMail was the first graphics-based e-mail system, allowing embedded, visible, clickable graphics. After selling 50,000 machines, NeXT was slimmed down to emphasize software design, then was sold back to Apple in November 1996.

Although by most traditional business measures, NeXT was a failure, it did allow Steve Jobs to refine and mature his leadership style, not to mention nourish his creative side. NeXT was a great place to work for both Steve and his employees, and it served as a valuable step and a new beginning in Steve's path forward.

He pretty much said that himself in his 2005 Stanford commencement address, in the now-famous quote: "I didn't see it then, but it turned out that getting fired from Apple was the best thing that could have ever happened to me. The heaviness of being successful was replaced by the lightness of being a beginner again, less sure about everything. It freed me to enter one of the most creative periods of my life."

MORE THAN A TOY STORY

It wasn't part of Steve's grand plan, but because of a divorce settlement, the graphics group in George Lucas's successful Lucasfilm company came up for sale in 1986 for $10 million. Jobs bought it with the vision of developing high-end graphics hardware. The graphics hardware never really took off as a salable product, but then the company got a huge break.

Pixar had been making some well-regarded shorts, like "Luxo Jr.," the familiar short starring two emotional Luxo lamps. It was mainly a demo for the Pixar Image Computer, which hadn't been doing very well. But Steve felt that Pixar was never really going to gain traction as it was and looked for something bigger. John Lasseter, a former Disney animator working for Pixar, had come up with some storyboards for a longer animated film called *Tin Toy*. He made a short that Jobs really liked and took a chance on, funding it out of his own pocket. Jobs and Lasseter went to Disney to sell Disney on a one-hour TV show based on this and similar animations, and were surprised to find that Disney saw it instead as a full-length feature film.

From that eventually came the blockbuster hit *Toy Story*. There were some production glitches and some contentious moments with Disney, but the film, released in 1995 after five years of development, was a huge hit. It redefined Pixar as a movie producer, not just a hardware producer. Pixar has released more than a dozen feature-length films since then, and the studio has never lost money. In 2006, Jobs sold his interest in Pixar to Disney for $7.4 *billion* in Disney stock, making him the company's largest shareholder.

In his Pixar role, Steve was more the business leader than the creative leader, handling the negotiations and dealings with Disney. He pretty much left the creative people alone to do their thing, something he didn't normally do when it came to a hardware product. Although many pundits question his trust of his workers, Steve hired good people and put a lot of faith in their talent and decision-making abilities, especially when he was dealing with topics he didn't know so much about.

BACK TO THE FUTURE: STEVE RETURNS TO APPLE

Apple went through sort of a "dark ages" period from the time Steve left in 1985 until his return in late 1996. The company tried to leverage the Macintosh platform into several flavors, sizes, and shapes. The only success among these launches was the PowerBook, a powerful but still heavy laptop version of the Mac. The product provided portability, networking capabilities, and color to the still-being-defined laptop space, and served as a model for others to emulate.

But the Apple standard became increasingly marginalized during this period. It languished as Windows captured all the personal computer growth, especially with the blockbuster Windows 95 release and with much cheaper hardware because of the memory and powerful processors that had become available. Dell and Compaq pretty much owned the space, especially in the business world. Apple's response was to sue Microsoft for copying Lisa's graphical interface, but this never went forward. Eventually, after a series of product and marketing failures, Sculley was shown the door (by Markkula, actually).

Things were not improved by the efforts of the next two CEOs: Michael Spindler and Gil Amelio. The company actually lost money for three years, 1996 to 1998. Amelio chose to focus on cutting operating costs, which is rarely an effective strategy, especially at a creative and innovative enterprise. The company struggled to enter other markets, like the PDA market, with Newton, another expensive failure. But he did have the vision to see the NeXT operating system as a good core for the next generation of Macintoshes. Apple also got Steve Jobs back as part of the $429 million deal.

Everyone could see the writing on the wall—except Amelio. Soon he was also ousted by a board that was frustrated by bland business results and a low stock price.

Steve Jobs took over as "interim" CEO ("iCEO," as many pundits, including Steve, referred to it) after being an energetic advisor for a while.

It's hard to imagine today, but Apple was really on the ropes in 1997. It had too many products, and most of them were just incremental, warmed-over versions of Mac desktops and laptops. It had failed with Newton. Its stock price was languishing. It had a small following, mostly of graphic designers, students, and teachers. There was no killer app. The operating system was aging and not particularly compelling. Software was limited, and many titles that hadn't been developed on the Mac didn't run well on it. Its dealer network was fading. And Windows was eating its lunch.

The company was now producing and cataloging 15 product platforms and thousands of variations among those platforms. Steve immediately saw this as a fundamental problem, one of lack of focus and poor strategic direction. It was like throwing a bunch of things at a wall to see what would stick—not a formula for success anywhere in business, and especially not in technology. Steve saw it as an extension of the battle for shelf space—lots of products, but not particularly good products; quantity instead of quality. This was not good for the products themselves, not good for the channel, not good for the brand, and, most of all, not good for the customer. And it was not good for profitability, as it required too many resources, spread too thin.

So Steve slashed and burned. He looked at the market as a very simple four-quadrant grid. One dimension was Customer, divided into Consumer and Professional. The other dimension was Product, divided into Desktop and Portable. He wanted one platform for each of the four quadrants and nothing more. Using this approach, by the end of 1998, he had whittled 350 specific products down to 10. The Steve Jobs Leadership Model was about to bloom, and Apple was about to take over the world.

I'll Have an iMac

At about the same time, the Internet was becoming all the rage, not only in the business world, but also for consumers. Steve Jobs had a vision for a bold new design for a new "all-in-one" computer with brightly colored side panels, an optical drive, a USB port, *no* floppy drive, and a "back that looked better than the front of everyone else's." The design details were taken care of by the renowned British-born industrial designer Jonathan Ive in a secret lab.

The iMac was a bold statement at a time when computers had become really boring beige boxes. It was designed for considerable eyeball appeal in a retail setting, was cool all over, and celebrated the change to a new millennium.

It worked, and it sold well. It got top praise from reviewers and critics. The iMac and its descendants, coupled with the revamped and highly visual OS X operating system introduced in 2000, returned Apple to its leading role in personal computing design, if not in terms of numbers, at least in terms of the appreciation of its loyal and growing audience.

And what is the "i" in iMac? When the iMac was first released, Apple claimed that it stood for "internet." That's plausible, but it also more tacitly represents its positioning as an "individual" or personal device. The brand strength of this single lowercase letter proved enormous in the marketplace.

It also gave a hint of a not-too-distant vision and the beginnings of Apple's transformation from a computer company into a digital company. On deck: the iPod.

THE VISION GETS A SOUNDTRACK

At the height of the dot-com boom, a small tremor was felt in the world of recorded music. It was called Napster, and for the first time, it allowed people to download and share music off the Internet—for free. It was cumbersome, and it was later determined to be illegal. But it could be done.

Steve Jobs noticed this. And Steve Jobs had long been a lover of music. He saw quite clearly that music would go digital some day. He thought about the current customer experience—what it was and what it should be.

Reliable downloads. Simple technology. Personal, convenient design. Easy shopping for new tunes. Fair revenues and profits for the sellers involved. It was a fairly obvious vision (in hindsight), but the current state of the art was far from it.

Fast forward: the iPod was the happy result. A tiny 1.8-inch hard disk drive had been developed by Toshiba in Japan. It was a solution looking for a problem, and Steve and Apple thought they had the problem. The few music players that had been made before that had relied on memory chips, so they couldn't hold very many songs. They certainly couldn't hold an entire music library.

Innovation is synthesis. Customers would want a device that could store a lot of songs—an entire library was best. But the device had to have the battery power to last long enough to play more than a few. It had to download those songs quickly—in five seconds, not five minutes. Customers would want it to be simple—no fiddling with 10 buttons while trying to jog. And, they would want a simple, legal, relatively inexpensive one-stop shop to acquire their music.

What did Steve do? He put it all together to provide a complete solution. The 1.8-inch drive supplied the storage. A new battery supplied the juice. Another Apple product, the FireWire, provided the fast download. Now, what about the music store?

That took some ingenuity. Steve himself took on this last piece of the vision with a music industry that was already gun-shy about the idea of Internet downloads. He proposed the 99-cent sale price, which was cheap enough for most consumers to accept the value proposition of an easy and legal download, but rich enough to give the record labels an acceptable cut. It was a win-win, and it provided a massive revenue stream for Apple once the original product was sold.

It all came together for a late 2001 launch. Jobs played an instrumental role in putting the pieces together to solve a major customer pain. People didn't even know they had the pain, but when they started to use the iPod and iTunes, they figured it out and switched immediately. Sales to date exceed 300 million. The meteoric rise in the company's value began shortly thereafter. And most of us spend far less time listening to music on traditional hi-fi systems, and fewer still buy packaged CDs these days.

ONE-BUTTON SUCCESS: THE IPHONE

The success of the iPod emboldened Steve and his team to take on another big customer challenge: the mobile phone. Customers hated their phones. Apple engineers hated their phones: they were ugly and too complex, with too many buttons, clunky retractable keyboards, not enough features, and not enough "cool."

To make a long story short, Apple engineers quickly designed an elegant, simple solution, the iPhone. It has one button. Like the iPod, it was a synthesis of iPod miniaturization and design, elements of the Mac OS, and excellent display, battery, and other hardware design.

And like the iPod, the real win was in developing the "ecosystem" around the phone—in this case, the "app." A huge network of developers, now numbering more than 100,000, saw the compelling platform and immediately went to work designing apps. There are more than 500,000 apps available through Apple's app store. The apps support the phone; the phone supports the apps. This symbiotic relationship hasn't come close to being matched elsewhere (Google is trying with its Android OS) and provides an enormous competitive advantage.

It also provided the basis to go one step further.

PUTTING IT ALL TOGETHER: THE IPAD

You have apps. You have an app store. You have iTunes. You have excellent display technology. You have excellent touch-screen technology. You have an increasingly visual, increasingly connected world, with Wi-Fi almost everywhere and 3G service where it isn't. There are e-books and e-book readers already out there. There are games and plenty of other electronic content in the form of newspapers, magazines, and so forth. And you have a customer base that is weary of the complexity, the form factor, the long boot-up times, the size and weight, the reading position, and the relative inconvenience of the laptop PC. And that customer wants to be connected in real time, as much as possible, from almost anywhere.

What would you do? What did Steve do?

Bring to market the iPad, that's what. It was almost a no-brainer after the iPod and the iPhone.

People thought it was so cool that they lined up outside Apple Stores everywhere to look at it. People could browse the Web, watch videos, read a book or a newspaper, or play a game from almost anywhere, and it was real easy. There was no mouse and no physical keyboard; you didn't need a table or flat surface to use it.

Most customers didn't know they needed one until they saw it. They were sold at first sight.

The iPad has become the mainstream consumer and business Web access device, while the PC has been relegated to a niche role for things that PCs do well—storing lots of data, writing and producing big reports and PowerPoints, and doing other more comprehensive tasks. Some people have to do that sort of thing some of the time, but the iPad captures what most people do with computers *most* of the time. It was a brilliant epiphany and a synthesis of what was already there—to the credit of Apple and the leadership of Steve Jobs.

AGAINST THE GRAIN: ACHIEVING EXCELLENCE IN RETAIL

Ever since the first Apple Is flew off the shelves at The Byte Shop in Mountain View, California, Apple had marketed its products through the retail channel. Over time, Apple had created a network of authorized and exclusive Apple dealers, and by the late 1990s, it had also begun to sell through the "big-box" chains such as CompUSA and Best Buy.

The dealer network had served Apple fairly well, but it was beginning to struggle as Apple's fortunes struggled in the mid-1990s. Computers were becoming less of a specialty item, and customers had started shopping more on price and selection—and they wanted to shop the choice between Apple and the booming Windows PC standard. The growth component of the industry migrated toward the big-box retailers.

The problem was, the kind of people these chains hired to work their floor weren't likely to be experts on computing, and were even less likely to be experts on Apple and Apple products. They were salespeople, and their objective was to move boxes. They didn't really care what brand they sold.

No Used-Car Salespeople, Please

Meanwhile, in the late 1990s, the PC manufacturer Gateway had set up its own retail channel in an effort to differentiate its brand and market its service and buying assistance as an extension of its whole product. At first these stores did quite well, particularly in combination with the company's friendly, down-home dairy cow trademarking and its South Dakota roots. But soon this concept wore out; Gateway moved its headquarters to San Diego, the cows went away, and the company lost its edge. People wanted to comparison-shop all PC choices for price, and to test-drive and buy printers and other accessories along with their PC; all this drove customers away from the Gateway stores and toward the big-box retailers.

Steve Jobs didn't like the big-box experience, as he thought it was detrimental to the Apple brand. He likened it to the used-car-buying experience, where customers had the "deal of the day" shoved down their throats. There was no connection with a brand, except perhaps the retailer itself, and there wasn't much connection there. Steve looked at the buying experience as an extension of the whole product, and he wanted control of that experience to make it a positive and to increase emotional involvement with the Apple brand.

Steve wanted a retail format that would enrich people's lives—an obvious extension of the product philosophy.

The "Think Different" Retail Store

When Steve Jobs disclosed his intentions to start the Apple Retail Store chain in the year 2000, most industry experts were doubters. They had witnessed the failure of the Gateway stores. They felt that Apple would have to make a painfully large investment in such brick-and-mortar facilities when the dot-com boom and the success of big-box retailers suggested a different course. Steve stuck to his guns.

Steve was pretty sure he wanted to do this, but he didn't want to make the same mistakes that Gateway had. He also recognized that he was no expert at retail, and so—for the first and only time at Apple—he hired consultants to help show him the way. He also recruited two of the more visionary retail experts at the time: former Target executive Ron Johnson, who had previously brought designer Michael Graves in to add a differentiating elegance to Target products, and former Gap CEO Mickey Drexler. Drexler joined the board of directors; Johnson became the manager of the retail operations.

Johnson, Jobs, and the retail team worked hard to design a differentiating elegance into the Apple Store format. They went for a clean, well-lighted, uncluttered look, with some of the same material and design touches found on Apple products: bright white surfaces; touches of metal in the right places; elegant, simple lines. They wanted customers to be able to experience the product, so all floor samples were up and running and connected to the Internet (compare that to your typical retail experience today!). Famously, Steve got very involved in the design and function of these stores, being particular about every element from floor to ceiling (literally).

Products were grouped by function, which at the time was the four-quadrant grid that Jobs had laid out upon his 1997 return: Desktop or Portable, Consumer or Professional. When the first Apple Stores opened in May 2001, the iPod wasn't even out yet, so the Apple Store had only the computer lines, most eye-catchingly the colorful iMac, to display.

A nice touch came in the form of the "Genius Bar," the concierge-style desk at the back of the store patterned after a similar feature found in the luxury chain Four Seasons hotel lobbies. Another nice touch was dispensing with the traditional cash registers and checkout lines found in most retail stores in favor of portable wireless devices carried by floor personnel. These personnel could deliver a personal shopping and consultation experience throughout the entire store visit. The obvious point was to give customers a complete and holistic presale and postsale product experience.

To make a longer story short, no other computer experience has even come close to the success of the Apple Store. The 357 stores open worldwide (as of July 2011) have become hubs of activity and destination locations in many shopping malls around the country. They have required crowd-control measures when new products, such as the iPad, were introduced. The resulting expansion of the Apple brand and customers' willingness to pay a higher price has produced incalculable value for Apple Inc.

The Apple Stores are a pure example of Steve's innovative spirit and his vision and passion for the customer experience. They represent a pure example of his leadership style.

"UNFORTUNATELY, THAT DAY HAS COME . . ."

Steve Jobs passed away peacefully on October 5, 2011, of respiratory failure related to the spread of pancreatic cancer.

Just prior to that, on August 24, 2011, Steve had announced his resignation as CEO, although he stayed on as board chairman. In his words: "Unfortunately, that day has come where I can no longer meet my duties and expectations as Apple's CEO."

Steve Jobs's declining health and the events leading up to his resignation and passing are widely known and documented. In mid-2004, he announced that he had been diagnosed with a rare but unusually treatable form of pancreatic cancer, and after undergoing alternative diet-based treatments for nine months, underwent a complex tumor-removal operation known as the Whipple procedure in July 2004.

The initial results were positive, and although he lost some weight and had a gaunt appearance at times, he delivered the famous 2005 Stanford commencement address in style and hung in as an active CEO for the next three years, giving the various keynote addresses and other presentations he had become so well known for. Speculation about his health continued through the end of 2008, when Steve announced that the January 2009 Macworld keynote address would be delivered by marketing VP Phil Schiller.

During that January, Steve disclosed that "[his] health issues were more complex than [he] originally thought." He took a six-month medical leave, during which he underwent a liver transplant. He returned from the leave with an excellent health prognosis, and while the speculation continued, he carried out his normal duties as Apple CEO.

In January 2011, he announced another medical leave without giving specific reasons. Despite this, he returned to launch the iPad 2 and give the keynote at the Worldwide Developer's Conference. He even gave a short talk and did a question-and-answer session with the Cupertino City Council in June 2011 to review plans for an enormous new headquarters facility (called a "spaceship" because of its circular form) to be built on property acquired from Hewlett-Packard in Cupertino, where that company had operated one of its largest sites. He looked underweight but otherwise appeared normal.

The rest is history. Apparently Steve knew his destiny, for he had authorized (and, some reports say, commissioned) journalist and former CNN CEO Walter Isaacson to do a 650-page biography. According to Isaacson, Jobs explained why he had authorized the work in a final interview shortly before his death. "I wanted my kids to know me," said Jobs. "I wasn't always there for them, and I wanted them to know why and understand why I did what I did."

He probably knew his destiny in the following often-quoted passage from the 2005 Stanford commencement address:

Remembering that I'll be dead soon is the most important tool I've ever encountered to help me make the big choices in life. Because almost every-

thing—all external expectations, all pride, all fear
of embarrassment or failure—these things just fall
away in the face of death, leaving only what is truly
important. Remembering that you are going to die
is the best way I know to avoid the trap of thinking
you have something to lose. You are already naked.
There is no reason not to follow your heart.

If nothing else, Steve Jobs followed his heart.

As leaders, we will all be well served to follow Steve
Jobs.

CHAPTER 3

MODEL

Democracies don't make great
products—you need a competent tyrant.

—Jean-Louis Gassée, former Apple VP,
Product Development

The Steve Jobs Leadership Model is above and beyond. The results make this clear. Its veneration and idolatry by the financial press, innovation specialists, tech gurus, and most of the consumer world make it abundantly clear.

So what's the difference between it and the same-old same-old that seems to be practiced all across corporate America (or the world, for that matter)? What's the special secret sauce that makes the Jobs model work, and work so much better than what so many have learned in business school, and what so many have learned on the job? How does "good" become "great"? How did Jobs lead 40,000 people to do the right thing, time after time, and be so happy about it and ready to do it again? Why is it that no other product-creating organization of 40,000 or more has been able to create and produce so much shareholder value?

Did Jobs put a dent in the traditional leadership model? If so, how?

ALL LEADERS ARE TYRANTS

The questions just posed are what we, as students of Steve Jobs's leadership, really need to get to. And the Jean-Louis Gassée quote cited at the beginning of the chapter goes a long way toward getting there. It goes a long way toward defining what the Jobs leadership style is all about, why it works, and how it's different.

Would the Apple "democracy" have succeeded without Jobs? Chances are, it would not have. We don't really have to speculate on that; we saw it clearly in Apple's dwindling fortunes, declining brand, and bland product offerings during his 11-year absence between 1985 and 1996.

And the "product"? That can be a small "p" (the product itself, the thing that comes in a box and is plugged into a wall by its purchaser), or it can be a large "P," representing a line of products, or, for all intents and purposes, a business. Either way, the history of commerce is littered with products designed by democracies ("camels designed by committees") that don't work.

Now, let's consider the second part of the quote.

I'll blurt this out: *all leaders are tyrants*. Some are just more competent than others.

For some leaders, tyranny is a daily occurrence. For others, it's more of a backup style, a fallback posture that is invoked when the going gets tough. But all leaders are tyrants. The difference is intent. The difference is really *why* they're being tyrannical. Is it about money and power? Is it about controlling other people, staying on top, and taking all the credit? Or is it about achievement and accomplishment and drive to realize a vision? It makes a huge difference.

And about that competence thing—we've all seen how competence and success can meet and override other unpleasant matters. There's the leader who knows what he is doing and inspires confidence. And then there's the leader who doesn't know what he is doing, is in over his head, and grabs on to the power of his position as an excuse to belittle the troops. While both may get immediate results, we know which one will win in the long term.

Competence wins. And as we've learned with Steve Jobs, competence with a bit of tyranny thrown in actually gains respect, rallies the troops, and gets it all done faster.

BUTTON-DOWN DEFINITIONS OF LEADERSHIP

The business schools and most business books on leadership all have variations on a fairly simple formula for leadership. Of course, they're a bit dry, and (not surprisingly) as we'll see, Steve Jobs took a different tack.

These models and manuals are crafted for current and aspiring managers, and they typically include both the *social* aspects of influencing others to get things done and the *structural* aspects of getting things done in an organization.

Business definitions of leadership usually center on the transactional and the transformational aspects of leadership. The *transactional* aspects of getting a task done with a group include planning, organizing, measuring, communicating, course correcting, and rewarding the team, all of which might be called task influence. The *transformational* aspects concern setting visions, generating ideas, motivating the team, stimulating creative thinking, and representing and "branding" the team to the outside world, all of which might be called social influence.

There are dozens of variations, but much of what is taught boils down to a sequence of actions designed to define a group, define a goal for that group, communicate the goal to the group, empower and motivate the group to get it done, and communicate the group's success inward and outward:

- *Planning.* The first thing to do is to decide what the goal is and how to get it done, usually as a combined individual and team effort. The goal should be specific, understandable, and measurable. Whether it is a business project or a hike in the forest, a leader maps out the task and the time frame, determines the steps along the way, and gets buy-in from the troops.
- *Organizing.* Once you have the goal, you organize your team effectively to get there. This includes recruiting, training, delegating, and communicating the goals, objectives, tasks, and timeline. Everybody

is given, or agrees to, a specific task and time frame, and resources are provided to accomplish the goal. A project is staffed correctly. Those hikers all know what they're supposed to bring on the trip.

- *Motivating*. Here the leader clarifies the benefits of accomplishing the group task, and any individual benefits that might go along with them. The leader works both one-on-one and with the group to remove roadblocks, empower the group, and get the team to think about the group success and *want* to put effort into it. Everyone is enthusiastic about the project and knows what's in it for her and for the business; the hikers are excited about getting to their destination and consider it worth the sweat and mosquito encounters involved.

- *Controlling*. While this term sounds more like an onerous and heavy-handed personality trait, it is really about staying on top of the situation, measuring results, making course corrections, communicating those corrections, and reinforcing the motivation where necessary to keep the project (or the hike) on track.

- *Communicating*. Once the project or task is completed, the results are communicated to the team and outside the team. This is where the marketing and evangelism usually come in, but they can be sprinkled throughout the process.

Along the way, a good leader should adopt and use personality traits to help smooth the task and social processes, including being authentic, empathetic, sensitive, and considerate. The effective leader puts himself in the shoes of those who are being led, rather than exercising position power and staying aloof, above, and beyond.

You might think this all sounds pretty "corporate," and it does. It looks like a process, not a culture. In fact, many corporate cultures speak of the process of management and the process of leadership. Steve Jobs, and other visionary leaders, did not look at leadership as a process. That's probably where the biggest difference lies—and where the most important lessons lie.

A Different Drummer

Steve Jobs turned these traditional models sideways. He did not follow either the structure or the sequence of the typical organizational or corporate approach. His model was not a process, or at least not the kind of process that most of us are used to.

Steve's style was far more focused, more detail-driven, and more evangelical. It built on a customer and product vision, and a strong innovation culture and mindset to get things done that had already been put in place. The employees in a Steve Jobs organization responded almost subconsciously to his influence and charisma.

That influence and charisma came from a unique ability to visualize the customer and the product, an unusual passion for detail, and a brilliant track record. But Steve didn't stop at just being a visionary.

Unlike most visionaries, he also took ownership of the project and the products, got into the details, and executed. These latter traits went a long way to establish his *competence*.

Steve started with the customer, created a vision, and built, nourished, and perfected an innovation culture within his organization (Steve Wozniak originally, and a cast of thousands eventually). With that context in place, *then* he defined the task (a product in many cases), built passion in the team and in the marketplace to get it all done, and then sold it.

The strength of Steve's vision and passion and the innovation culture that was already in place made the generation of group passion, and eventually the task, and ultimately the sale, much easier.

THE "TYRANT" PART

And yes, there was bound to be a little "tyranny" along the way. In most cases, that tyranny appeared to be merely a manifestation of Steve's passion, used occasion-ally to keep the creative forces flying in formation. It was rarely, if ever, a raw exercise of power for power's sake. It was a tyranny of competence, not a tyranny of power. There's a big, big difference between the two.

Not only did Steve depend on his own competence, but he went the extra mile to instill that competence, and expect it, in his team. "My job is not to be easy on people. My job is to pull things together from different parts of the company and clear the ways and to get the resources for the key projects. And to take these great people we have and push them and make them even better, coming up with more aggressive visions of how it could be."

Clearly, this was not a message of self-interest, but one of achievement of a greater good and a greater goal for the organization. It also recognized the importance of vision. But this message and others like it have been interpreted over time as being heavy-handed, "auto-cratic," "manipulative," and "boorish." Many people who have worked for Steve have related experiences of his being temperamental, mercurial, and unapproachable. But most employees, from top to bottom, found him easy to work with and supportive—if you were with the program and doing the right work.

The Flip Side

Still, there are numerous reports of his dysfunctional or just plain nasty treatment of subordinates. Many of these reports came forth in what amounted to a career eulogy for Jobs after his departure from Apple, announced in August 2011.

According to *New York Times* reporter Joe Nocera, in comments made upon the departure based on an interview years ago: "He was not a consensus builder but a dictator who listened mainly to his own intuition. He was a maniacal micromanager." And: "He could be absolutely brutal in meetings: I watched him eviscerate staff members for their 'bozo ideas.'"

CNN Money's Peter Elkind described an almost binary approach to the world: ideas, products, and work were either "insanely great" or "shit"; as an employee, you were either a "genius" or a "bozo," a frequently used term for someone who didn't get the program or, worse, got in the way or "tried to push something not in the best customer interest." And it could change in a flash; these flips were described by Apple employees as his "hero-shithead roller coaster."

Frederick Allen, writing for *Forbes* and citing Nocera's comments in an article titled "Steve Jobs Broke Every Leadership Rule. Don't Try This Yourself," describes Apple's "ruthless corporate culture [as] just one piece of a mystery that virtually every business executive would love to understand," then goes on to ask, "How does Apple do it?"

Allen postulates, quite correctly, that it's all about vision and genius—competence, that is—with a healthy dose of charisma thrown in. "Go ahead and behave the way he did yourself, as a CEO—as long as you've got all of Steve Jobs' charisma, revolutionary vision, and innovative genius, along with relentless drive and temper."

All of this reinforces the "competent tyrant" image.

RULE MAKER, RULE BREAKER

The Motley Fool, a popular investing website (www.fool.com), has stimulated individual investors' thinking for years by promoting two simultaneous investing approaches: a "Rule Maker" and a "Rule Breaker" portfolio. The Rule Maker portfolio follows all the standard investment criteria: it takes a value approach, examining the usual things that are aligned with a company's intrinsic value. Buy a Rule Maker, and you'll do well over time. But will you get "insanely great" results? Probably not.

The Rule Breakers are stocks that don't follow the rules, but that have a certain something about them that makes the whole greater than the sum of its parts. They look ahead. They look over the horizon. They have a story; the intangibles and the certain something about them ultimately create more value than the fundamentals that are already on paper.

Rule Breakers are usually "think different" companies, revolutionary companies that don't follow the rules today but will ultimately rule their universe and their markets. They get higher stock valuations (as measured by their price/earnings ratio and other such measures) and aren't scrutinized so much for their fundamentals because of that—the fundamentals will come later. As companies go, Apple, Google, and a limited handful of others would qualify today, as Microsoft, Starbucks, and others have done in the past.

We're talking about companies here, but as a leader, naturally Steve Jobs could be described as a Rule Breaker—or as someone who merely followed his own rules.

AYN RAND MEETS STEVE JOBS

Well, I don't believe such a meeting ever actually happened—but it sure would have been interesting if it had. If you search for a definition of Rule Breaker on the Motley Fool site, you come to a quote adapted from Ayn Rand's epic novel *The Fountainhead*, adapted by Edwin Locke in his book *The Prime Movers*:

> The great creators—the thinkers, the artists, the scientists, the inventors—stood alone against the men of their time. . . . Every great new invention was denounced. . . . But the men of unborrowed

vision went ahead. They fought, they suffered and they paid. But they won. . . .

Men have been taught that it is a virtue to agree with others. But the creator is the man who disagrees. Men have been taught that it is a virtue to swim with the current. But the creator is the man who goes against the current. Men have been taught that it is a virtue to stand together. But the creator is the man who stands alone. . . .

The creator—denied, opposed, persecuted, exploited—went on, moved forward and carried all humanity along on his energy.

Surely, Steve Jobs is a pretty ideal example of one of these creators. Did he "carry all humanity along on his energy"? Sure seems that way.

A DEFINITION STEVE WOULD HAVE LIKED

We could talk about Steve's personality, style, and success all day, but that's not really why you bought this book, is it? The point is to try to get to the essence of Frederick Allen's question: "How does Apple do it?" Or, more to the point, "How did Steve do it?"

To begin with, I think it helps to get back to what, at its essence, leadership really *is*. Many people have offered complex explanations of what leadership is, what it does, and what personality traits it requires; we could spend a lot of time on it.

Or, we can go with a simple, back-to-basics definition that I think Steve would have liked:

> Leadership is getting people to want to, and to be able to, do something important.

It's worth taking a minute to analyze the three components of this definition. The last phrase, "do something important," is critical, for people are more likely to rally around doing something important; moreover, if people put a lot of effort into things that turn out *not* to be important, they will quickly stop investing in those efforts.

Many leadership definitions contain the "want to" aspect, the idea that good leaders don't work through coercion, but rather work through motivation. People who want to do something, whether for psychic or financial rewards or both, are likely to do it better and do it faster.

However, many leaders forget that individuals and teams must be provided with the tools and resources to get it done, and that the leaders must clear the path and remove roadblocks. Individuals and teams want resources and support, and guidance when they need it.

And many leaders mistakenly rely more on coercion than on motivation to get employees to want to do something. Coercion makes people feel that they *have* to do something, not that they *want* to. When this happens, they rarely feel good about doing something until it's done, and even that good feeling doesn't last long. Although Apple employees generally do well financially and have a pleasant work environment, the company genererally has not used that kind of incentive to move people and projects. Instead, most employees subscribe to the vision and want to become part of something great.

This idea reached its zenith when the iPod became its own reward—the people working on the project made the extra effort not for stock options and bonuses, but because they wanted one!

The three elements of the definition work in balance: great things happen only if teams are aligned to want to accomplish something important and have the means to do so. Within this definition, Steve did what he could to provide the vision, the tools, and the environment to do something really great.

What would Steve have done? One, figure out something that was really important to do. Two, communicate this vision, provide a solid team environment, and make sure that people share the desire to get it done.

Three, provide the resources and remove the roadblocks standing in the way.

ACHIEVEMENT, NOT MONEY AND POWER

Over the years, Steve gained a lot of respect from those inside and outside the company by maintaining a focus on achievement, despite his fame and the fortune he gained through his enterprises. He rarely, if ever, talked about money, and aside from a few pieces of choice real estate, he did not get caught up in the trappings of wealth. Steve was one of the most influential business leaders on the planet, yet for the most part, he didn't use his power to meddle in politics or in the affairs of other individuals or companies. Except for his product presentations, Steve kept a fairly low profile and lived more like the rest of us than most people with his elevated stature.

This was in clear contrast to most executives and CEOs these days, who seem to favor money and power over plain old achievement.

For Steve Jobs, achievement was the goal. Money and power were the result. That was true both for him personally, and for the company he led.

Are you achievement-motivated? Or are you power-motivated? Think about it.

THE ZEN OF RESPECT

For most effective leaders, what it comes down to at the end of the day is *respect*. Plain old R-E-S-P-E-C-T, as Aretha Franklin sang out so clearly. Leaders who have earned the respect of their followers are far more likely to be willingly followed. Their goals are more likely to be assumed to be important. The means to accomplish these goals are more likely to be put in place. Most of all, the team will be more willing to contribute. Respect breeds trust, trust breeds respect, and the cycle continues.

Respected leaders get chances to fail, because they know that most of their efforts will result in success. They get people to follow them even if those followers don't 100 percent understand the vision. They get the benefit of the doubt, and the benefit of the doubt can be a huge tailwind when someone is leading a large organization through uncertain waters. Respected leaders also tend to respect and trust their followers. When leaders respect their followers and followers respect and trust their leaders, the gates are open for success.

Steve Jobs was a follower of Zen, and Zen is all about attaining enlightenment, and feeling whole, through the wisdom of experience. Respect is also gained through the wisdom of experience, and Steve Jobs deployed the political capital of respect to its fullest extent.

But as we all know, respect is difficult to achieve, and it is usually not achieved through deliberate efforts, which are typically rebuffed by others as being transparent and self-serving. Respect must come naturally and organically with time.

Here are four of the principal ways in which Steve Jobs obtained the respect of his employees, the tech industry, and the consuming public.

RESPECT THROUGH VISION

Steve repeatedly demonstrated that he could see just a little bit farther than everybody else, and could create products that exceeded customer expectations and defined customer experiences that the customers themselves didn't even know they desired. This "guru" capability is one of the greatest—and most difficult to emulate—sources of respect. As we'll explore later in the book, if you stay close enough to the customer and keep an innovation mindset, that won't automatically guarantee a winning vision or a winning execution, but it will make it more likely to happen.

RESPECT THROUGH DETAIL

Workers generally love a leader who understands what they are doing and who can get into the trenches with them. They feel that the leader can empathize with them and with their struggles to get a job done. They trust the leader, and the leader trusts them, so long as they stay on task. And if they get stuck, the leader can provide meaningful direction to solve their problems.

Even John Sculley later recognized one of the qualities of visionary leaders that Steve clearly had: "to be so in touch with the internal details that when something isn't working, they have the leadership talent to adjust in flight."

Respect through Accomplishments

This one almost goes without explanation. Steve was right so many times about the product and its market, and he built, well, the world's most valuable publicly traded company, so it's pretty hard not to respect him for that.

Respect through Being the Face of the Product

When a leader is so "all-in" behind and into a product, and a company, that he is willing to be its public presence, its public face, and part of its brand, that's a compelling add-on to the aura of leadership and respect that's already out there. We've seen it before with the likes of Lee Iacocca and to a lesser extent with Herb Kelleher of Southwest Airlines, Dave Thomas of Wendy's, and others. They live, breathe, evangelize, and are totally connected to their product and its experience.

Leaders like Iacocca are probably involved in all phases of product development (as Iacocca was with the Chrysler K-Car platform) and follow by being the chief spokesman. These kinds of connections and efforts go above and beyond the normal call of duty. They show connections to the product, not personal grandeur, which go a long way toward building respect from the troops, not to mention the customer.

THE RIGHT HAND FOR THE LEFT HAND

Steve Jobs was left-handed. That may not surprise most of you who typically associate left-handed people with alternative or contrarian thinking. But that's not the point here.

The point is that even Steve Jobs recognized his limitations. While Steve had a mind for detail to the extreme when it came to customers and products, he didn't align well with the administrative details of running a big company. Although evidence suggests that he often knew the financials better than the financial people, and that he demanded financial perfection just as he demanded product perfection, the financials weren't really his bag.

So throughout Steve's career, he always had a strong "right-hand" person taking care of the details of running a large, publicly held company and doing all that "other stuff" beyond product development and marketing. Mike Markkula, Mike Scott, and John Sculley were all brought on board as CEOs in the early days (remember, Steve was only 28 when Sculley was recruited). Jay Elliot served as a senior vice president and right-hand man well into the second phase of Apple's success after Jobs's return.

A good leader hires a good sidekick and places a lot of trust in that sidekick. They become "joined at the hip"—although they must be strategically aligned, something that obviously changed or was overlooked during the John Sculley years. A good visionary hires or partners with a strategically aligned nuts-and-bolts person to help him execute (Abraham Lincoln/Edwin Stanton, Bush/Cheney, and many others of far lower profile). This seems pretty simple, but it's amazing how many leaders (HP's Carly Fiorina comes to mind) think they can do everything, and fail when they try.

THE STEVE JOBS LEADERSHIP MODEL

It's pretty hard to structure a visionary. Visionaries, Steve Jobs included, defy structure. They act on instinct and experience, and what they do is hard to fit into a definitive model.

But we all need to learn from Steve; that's why this book came to be. So I will try to put a structure around what he did to help you grasp the essence of what made him great. Now, mind you, this isn't a "scouting manual" step-by-step leadership approach; rather, it is more of a thought process, a Zenlike state of being that you leaders out there can emulate, whether you are running a small work group or a Fortune 500 company.

Six Steps

Although Steve Jobs's leadership style defied conventional wisdom, I do see six critical elements, which can be loosely organized into steps that made him different, and that I believe he followed instinctively.

At the core of Steve's style and success was an unwavering focus on the customer and on the product. That in itself set Steve apart from many corporate leaders, who are more focused on organization and numbers stuff. Steve's focus on product is worth a book in and of itself, and indeed, several have been written on the history and style of Apple's innovation.

I do think Steve's customer and product focus are both unique and extraordinary. But what is equally extraordinary is the "connective tissue" he added in to get the product *done* and then *to market*.

As such, I see "Customer" (an intense scrutiny of the customer and the customer experience) as one unique piece of Steve's leadership, and I see "Product" as another and perhaps more obvious and transparent step. But what lies between Customer and Product?

It is in this gap where, in my view, many companies fail. They may know their customers pretty well (although I believe that most don't), and they may have good machines to produce products. But something gets lost in the translation. Interestingly, look at the successes and failures of the Japanese. As Steve was, the Japanese are very close to their customers and their customers' needs, and can produce excellent products. But the absence of the connective tissue between the two—the lack of creativity, the ability to see a holistic outcome, and a cultural reluctance to think differently—all together get in the way of the Japanese.

Where I believe Steve excelled—and what really made the Jobs difference—are the two steps between knowing the customer and producing a perfect, break-through product. Those steps are "Vision" (the translation of customer experience and needs into a product need and concept) and "Culture" (the creating and nurturing of an organizational innovation culture that actually can get things done and exceed everyone's expectations).

So now we have four "steps": Customer, Vision, Culture, and Product.

But products don't sell themselves, and Steve didn't stop there. He was an expert at launching and creating the buzz around his products—more so than anyone else in American corporate history. So there's another step, "Message," that included not only his message to the consuming public, but also the messages to his internal teams that kept them so motivated and on task and eager to tackle the next iProduct.

These five steps define the right product and get it to the right market, and normally I'd stop there, but I see one more thing that isn't really a "step" but more of a Steve Jobs protocol. It's a bit more abstract. I think Steve thought about, and continually perfected, his own personal brand (as well as the Apple brand; they went hand in hand). Good leaders get stuff done, but most of them don't seem to have the right approach to marketing themselves, their organizations, and their successes. Doing so builds and solidifies respect in the process, enabling them to go out and do it all over again. The building of the personal "Brand" perpetuates the success.

So now we have six "steps," or elements, of the Steve Jobs Leadership Model.

1. Customer
2. Vision

3. Culture
4. Product
5. Message
6. Brand

- *Customer.* Steve had a unique way of getting to what customers need by understanding what causes them pain today. Most organizations take the wrong approach (if they take any approach at all) to understanding what is really going on with their customers. Chapter 4 shows how Steve viewed the customer and the customer experience.
- *Vision.* Visionaries all have visions, of course. Steve Jobs had a unique way of tying customer needs and experiences to complete and holistic product and customer experience visions. Chapter 5 covers how Steve's "seeing over the horizon" visioning really worked, and how he spread his visions through his organization.
- *Culture.* Where the rubber really fails to meet the road in many organizations is in culture. Innovation is often set off in some ivory-tower R&D lab far from any other element of the company. It isn't part of everyday life for the company. Or, people are not rewarded for, or are even discouraged from, thinking outside the box. Chapter 6 shows how Steve built his organization through

recruiting and he irrigated an innovation mind-set within it.

- *Product.* Once we have the vision and the culture, we can start producing products. But are these products incremental tweaks or little white boxes that stop where they are plugged into an electric outlet? Nope. Chapter 7 describes how Steve and Apple conceived and developed holistic products that have been so successful that they define markets—and leave customers waiting for the next breakthrough.

- *Message.* Now that we have a product, we have to put the right message around it to get attention and convey its value. Steve's leadership didn't stop with creating a product; he brought it to market personally. He created more product excitement than any other business leader in history, and Chapter 8 gets to how that worked.

- *Brand.* Finally, in Chapter 9 we get to the more abstract notion of building your own *personal* brand and reputation, which creates the aura of respect and credibility that makes it easier for you to go out and do it, whatever "it" is, over and over again.

This six-step model becomes the framework for the remaining chapters of *What Would Steve Jobs Do?* I will take apart each of these steps and offer the "What Would Steve Jobs Do?" message in each, the idea being that someday they will also answer the question: "What Would *You* Do?"

CHAPTER 4

CUSTOMER

If I asked my customers what they wanted,
they'd have told me, "a faster horse."

—*Henry Ford*

The room was dark. The candy dish was full of M&Ms, and there was a dish of mixed nuts alongside it. In the back of the room was a tray of mini deli sandwiches, cheeses, and assorted vegetables—finger foods all ready for the taking. And of course, there was plenty of coffee, tea, juices, sodas, and water to go around.

The only light in the room came from the larger conference room in front of the glass. The glass was a large plate window of almost bulletproof thickness, a thickness so complete that hardly a sound passed other than what was miked into the room.

The fluorescence washed the room in bright white with a pale yellow-green cast. There was a large table with six people sitting around it. On the table was another plateful of snacks (not as nice as the ones on the "dark side" of the glass) and a couple of copies of the company's latest product.

The people in front of the glass, supposedly chosen at random from all walks of life, were asked how they use the company's product, in this case, a Windows PC. When the question came around to the lady in the salmon-colored dress at the far corner, with glasses and curly dishwater-blond hair, she smiled. "I have a dog who loves to run. When someone opens the front door, he's outa here. So I use my PC mainly to make 'lost dog' signs."

The dimly lit faces of the product marketing team behind the glass and the candy dishes were all smiles. A collective chuckle rang out. "That's a good one" was heard from one of the product managers in the corner. The chuckle died down quickly, and the questioning moved on to the next player. "I use my PC to run my household finances, and my kids use it to do their homework."

On and on the evening went. The group learned how their customers use the machine, and they took in a few frustrations with it—it doesn't boot up fast enough, it crashes occasionally while on the Internet, something about the software. On and on it went—along a road really to nowhere.

A DECENT BURIAL

Did the people on the product marketing team really learn anything? Did they get any real and actionable insight into the customer experience? Did they get the feedstock for any epiphanies about how customers use these products and what they *really* want?

Not likely. The members of the product marketing team went back to their hotel, slept off their late-evening snacks, and went for a nice breakfast in the morning. Did they know their customer any better? Probably not. They'd heard all the answers before. Did their senior managers know the customer better? Definitely not. They didn't even attend the focus group. And the report they read (if they read it at all) was watered down with corporate-speak so as to not be too disruptive, and to reinforce all the things that the company was doing right.

And of course, none of the people involved can act on anything they saw last night, because focus groups are not statistically significant; now they must do quantitative research.

The report may or may not have been read. It was filed with all the other reports. Whatever "ahas" might have come from that two-hour session were now buried in some file somewhere in the organization, probably never to be seen again. The organization validated what it could, and may have added a feature or a refinement here or there to solve a problem. And it moved on.

The marketing team—and the company—continued with the next product release in its product plan.

There were a few tweaks. Faster, cheaper, and better, but not different.

The customer got a faster horse.

The organization did what organizations usually do.

Did the marketing team really understand the customer? No. It checked a box—"we did research"—and moved on with the mainstream "mission" of the business.

FASTER HORSES DON'T MATTER

The story just told is true, although a lot of the details are missing. I was there, and it was a major Silicon Valley tech firm that conducted the research.

But those details aren't important. The point is that this kind of story happens over and over, and it's part of the reason why Apple is Apple, and everyone else is everyone else.

The "faster horse" quote was one of Jobs's favorites. If you ask a group of customers how to make a product better, they'll usually tell you what's wrong with it. The customers will tell you "from experience" that the horse is too slow.

Naturally, the product people will focus on designing a faster horse, without questioning whether a horse is the right product to begin with. The faster part is easier to work on than replacing the horse. Everybody understands the horse. It's easier to focus and concentrate on improving the horse.

Perhaps most of all, the organizational "antibodies," with all their reasons "why they can't," will rise up to attack any idea that takes the organization away from its cherished steed. In most organizations, these antibodies exist at all levels—including the leadership. The horses (the legacy technologies) stay in place and, at best, get bolt-on, incremental improvements.

Steve Jobs did things differently. He didn't take the horse for granted or see it as a given. The horse was in play. Faster, better, smoother, on less feed, and with fewer hours brushing in the stall would be nice, but what the customer really wanted was conveyance. Fast, yes, but also easy, dry, comfortable, reliable, cheap, less maintenance, longer range, carry passengers, easier to store—it's not hard to see now, but it took Henry Ford to see it then.

Apple and Steve Jobs, as well as Henry Ford, are famous for not hiring consultants, not doing traditional market research, and not listening to customers in the traditional way. What is it that they know that most of corporate America doesn't know?

What's Wrong with "Customer Intimacy"?

Customer intimacy—and all of its phraseological variants—was all the rage in the 1990s and 2000s. The 1980s fad for Japanese quality and manufacturing techniques gave greater impetus to the idea of really focusing on customers, watching them in action, and listening to what they want.

The Internet, of course, made this all the more possible, and soon, in the 2000s, we started to hear about "collaborative design" and "crowdsourcing," where the customer not only gave you feedback but became part of the process to help you design your product.

Customer intimacy implies a relationship with customers, a closeness that makes it possible to have a dialogue that enables you to understand the customer and the customer to understand you. As in any relationship, open lines of communication, patience, and listening can draw out some of the customer's inner thoughts about you, about your products, and about how you deliver and support your products. You, in turn, if you so choose, can take that information and do a better job of making the customer happy.

That's the standard construct, and for most businesses (and governments, schools, and other nonprofit organizations, for that matter), this is a good thing to do. These intimate contacts, if they are executed well and really used to deliver customer value, can't hurt and probably can help.

But there are some important limitations to the traditional "intimacy" approach. Intimacy can help you design better products and a better customer experience, but the resulting improvements are likely to be incremental. So long as you take the following shortcomings into account, intimacy efforts make sense. But don't expect them to pay off in the game-changing manner in which Steve Jobs has led Apple. Why not? Because no matter how intimate you are with your customers, they can't give you the insight you need to really change their world.

Customer Mindset

Listening to customers is great, but in most cases, you'll run into the following limitations:

- *Customers can see only where they've been.* As in the focus group session described at the beginning of the chapter, most customers are aware only of what they've experienced. Most customers are more aware of the shortcomings and pain of using your products than of the possibilities. You can listen in to hear their pain, especially if you can turn those micro "pain points" into larger class issues, but these customers won't tell you where to head next.
- *They can see only what they have, not what they don't have.* If someone asks you about your car, are you going to tell him about the one you have now? Or will you tell him about the one you'll have next? Aside from citing some feature that a competitor already has, can you or would you tell the carmaker what you don't have and would like to have? Customers tend not to see beyond your product and a competitor's product.
- *They don't see what they* could *have.* Again, customers don't see very far ahead; in addition, they don't know the technology (or the financials), and

they don't know what's possible. In Jobs's own words, "Customers don't know what they want until you show it to them."

Once again, these limitations don't mean that you shouldn't listen to your customers. It's just a question of what you can expect when you do—incremental tweaks, not game-changing results.

Wrong Customers

Most organizations talk the most, and listen the most, to their biggest and/or most mainstream customers. That makes sense intuitively: you talk to the people who butter your bread. But those are the people who are most used to, and most dependent on, your products. They're most likely to demand only small tweaks to the products. They're pretty happy with what they have already; if they weren't, they'd be someone else's customer, not yours, right? Worse, depending on what you're selling, since they buy a lot of it, they may be more concerned about lowering the price than about adding features to it.

The point is not to ignore this group, but to realize that new ideas and new markets may not originate here.

Wrong Time Frame

Customers operate in the past and in the here and now. They know what you sell. They know what the competition sells. However, they don't know what they will need five years from now, or even a year from now. More to the point, especially in a tech-driven business, they don't know or can't conceive what's possible.

In sum, customer intimacy will help you learn about your customers' pain, if you listen closely. But you need to fill in the gaps if you are to turn those pain points into a meaningful and actionable customer need. Fair warning: if you become *too* intimate with customers, you'll only tweak features and monkey with the price.

And you'll never deliver any positive surprises.

There's a "C" in Leadership

When you're at the helm, whether you're the CEO or a line supervisor in the shipping department, you need to thoroughly understand your customers. You can't let others, like consultants, do it for you, and you can't rely on your customers to tell you what they need. They may know what they need to get their next task done, but do they know what they *really* need to make their lives better?

What made Steve Jobs different? Did he understand technology better than everyone else? Did he understand better than everyone else how products work? Was he a better speaker than everyone else? Was he a better recruiter of talent than everyone else?

Maybe so. But what really set him apart was his understanding of the customer and his *passionate empathy* for the customer. He had the ability to turn customer needs—"deep" needs, "below the surface" needs that they don't even know they have—into solutions.

Quite simply, you can't provide solutions unless you know the problem. And Steve Jobs knew the "problem"—and defined it and articulated it—probably better than anyone else on the planet. That became his vision, which we will cover in the next chapter.

Intimate knowledge of the customer *is* often what sets exceptional enterprise leadership apart. Strong customer knowledge and a strong customer sense will help you and the organization make the right decisions. As we've learned with Apple and Steve Jobs, this customer expertise goes a long way toward establishing the respect and credibility that are so important to leading successfully. You know what to do, your employees know you know, and they know that they can depend on you to guide the ship toward the right results.

As a leader, you must become your customer's champion-in-chief for the organization. You have to be the customer spokesperson and representative. You have to visualize the customer and the customer experience, and drive everything from it. You are the focal point for your organization's customer sense.

You aren't the only person who needs to do this, however. Customer sense needs to happen at the bottom and middle tiers of your organization as well. But don't just delegate the task. The bottom and middle tiers can't develop this sense for you. If you turn it over to an organization, you'll get an "organization" solution. If you turn it over to outsiders, you'll get an "outsider" solution, one that is far distant from the soul of your enterprise.

SENSING YOUR CUSTOMERS

Steve Jobs didn't really have a process to develop his strong customer sense. He did it intuitively by thinking about customers and thinking about what *is* and what *could be* as a customer.

Jobs did these things very well, and, of course, we'd all like to be like Steve. But some of us mere mortals need a little more of a cookbook, a little more of a recipe and checklist to follow, especially as we redirect our sensibilities from our day-to-day organizational lives to the external world and "deep" customer needs.

I have made an attempt to bottle what Steve would do into three essential steps to develop that customer sense that *all* leaders should think about if they are to stay on board and out in front of their customers. Those components are:

- *See* the customer
- See the *experience*
- *Be* the customer

Let's take these items apart, one by one.

SEE THE CUSTOMER

That sounds pretty easy, doesn't it? Just watch or listen to your customers and try to understand who they are, what their experiences are, and what their needs are, right? Well, yes, but the devil is in the details.

You can quantify and segment your customers with surveys and all sorts of other metrics. You can watch your customers in action using a product or at a local store, although you must take care to avoid the spotlight—and the possible behavior changes that can be brought on by being in the spotlight.

These activities are a good start. But they only get to the surface of the customer. They might give you some insight into who your customers are and what they do with your products. But they don't get to the deep stuff—what your customers *think* and what they *could do* with products.

To get there, Steve and others really tried to get into a customer's mind—to think like a customer. They wanted to visualize all the customers out there: who they are, how they became customers, what they're thinking about the status quo, and what they're thinking about the competition. He directed his organization to do the same.

Once he asked his team: "Who is the largest education company in the world?" Apparently only two responders got it right: Apple. So special effort went into thinking about those customers, how they would view the status quo, and ultimately what they would want in a current or future Apple product.

Beyond these and other "core" customers, Jobs took a pretty wide view of who the customer is. Think about the customer on the fringe, not just the mainstream. Think about those people who aren't customers at all right now. How can digital technologies be used to make their lives better? A good example is the "fringe" customer in the late 1990s who was trying to get digital technologies to work to download music from the Internet. Being a music lover himself, Steve was fascinated by this possibility; it was something that could be done much better with digital technology, just as desktop publishing and computer graphics had been revolutionized years earlier.

A DAY IN THE LIFE OF ...

A young professional 30-something graphic designer living in an urban area and commuting to work by subway. A suburban homemaker and mother of two who runs a small tie-dyed shirt business on the side. A 42-year-old female teacher and part-time music instructor. A 75-year-old semiretired male business owner.

You've seen all these people, right? Sure. But you probably haven't explored their needs for computing or for digital media.

One tool that Apple teams use is the development of *customer personas*. Customer personas are small, simple biographical sketches of a "stereotype" customer and her typical behavior. These personas can be developed and storyboarded into an assortment of customer experiences and needs. They add a sense of realism and purpose to the process, more so than the usual segmentation exercises, which tend not to have more than four profiles to work with.

Some of these profiles are mainstream; some are at the fringes. From them, ideas can flow about what's wrong with, and what could be better about, a customer experience. It's amazing how few companies do this, relying instead on standard market segments like "producers," "technologists," and so forth.

Seeing the customer is the first step toward *thinking* like the customer. Once he had a vision of a target customer in mind, Steve and the team appraised that customer's experience and put on that customer's shoes in the interest of giving him a new, better, and previously unthought-of experience.

SEE THE *EXPERIENCE*

When you get right down to it, any product or service is an experience. That experience starts when a customer first notices your product, and it ends when she disposes of it or replaces it. Most companies have gotten "hip" to the idea of a "total customer experience," and see the elements of the experience, the "whole product," around the core product. But some do it better than others.

What differentiates Steve Jobs's and Apple's approach is the depth of their observation and the takeaways from the customer experience.

CUSTOMER PAIN

Steve and his design teams were well known for appraising the sources of customer pain and discontent with a given product or process. If an operating system would hang or cause confusion or would take too long to boot, if there were too many buttons on a cell phone, if there were too many steps in a music download process, Steve and his team noted those experiences right away.

This approach included assessing not only the pain associated with a product and its related processes, but also the pain felt by a customer persona. The team examined the persona protagonist's life, how well current products served his needs, and how future ideas and products could make his life better.

The April 2003 introduction of the iTunes music store is a great example of analyzing the "pain and pleasure" of a customer experience. During his presentation, Steve shared four benefits of the "status quo" music download experience at the time:

- Vast selection of music, "better than any record store on the planet"
- Unlimited CD burning
- Music could be stored on any MP3 player
- It's free!

But there was pain too, not only with the technology, but also from the fact that the downloads weren't really legal:

- Unreliable downloads (would shut down in midstream)
- Unreliable quality

- No previews
- No album cover art or other info
- "It's stealing"

He went on to suggest that "most people don't focus on these things," but looked at only the good stuff. These pain factors led to the historic negotiations with the music industry to create the 99-cent download and the iTunes software platform to download and manage music. Both new ideas, considered disruptive at the time, have become industry standards. In Steve's words: "Music downloads, done right."

SIMPLICITY VS. COMPLEXITY

Steve was a stickler for getting things simple and keeping them that way. Complex keyboard sequences, like Microsoft's ubiquitous "right-click" controls, drove him and the design team nuts. The nominal approach is, "How can we make something better by making it simpler?" Instead of arguing about how to construct user manuals, the team strives to make them obsolete. Ditto for "out-of-box experience" sheets to get customers started with a product.

The one-button iPhone is the best example, but all through the company's history, and especially since 2000, product physical and functional designs are simple, clean, straightforward, and clear. The team strives for "elegant simplicity," a concept that we'll take up again in Chapter 7.

Sensory Experience

Those of you readers who live on the West Coast are probably familiar with the regional chain of fast-food restaurants known as In-N-Out Burger. Founded in 1948 and still family-owned, with 258 locations in four states, In-N-Out sells a simple assortment of hamburgers and french fries. It has only four main-course items on the menu, in contrast to the dozens offered by competitors.

A hamburger joint? As a model for a sensory customer experience? It's pretty amazing, but it's true. And the lines of people waiting for their burgers at all hours of the day tells you it's something special.

The burgers are good and the fries are pretty good, but the sensory experience from start to finish is excellent. The sights, sounds, and smells are excellent. From the moment you get close, specially designed kitchen exhaust fans share the aroma with the nearby environs. When you walk in, the place is spotless, with a small crew cleaning up constantly. When you use the drive-through, large, high-quality audio components are used to take and play back your order—there's no scratchy miscommunication. The help is clean-cut, articulate, and smart (and paid more than most). If the workers get their white uniforms dirty on the job, they change to clean ones immediately. A large plate-glass window at the drive-through allows you to see everything that's going on in the kitchen. The french fries are cut from raw potatoes in plain sight.

Steve Jobs didn't run a hamburger joint, and we're all probably better off because of that. But if he had, In-N-Out would be a good model. Steve and his designers appreciated how products bring with them a sensory experience. In the case of Apple products, there is really no smell, but the sights, touches, and sounds are all of utmost importance. Any Apple design—including the box and the packaging—considers the sensory experience. The results are obvious for anyone who has bought, opened, and used an Apple product.

Using a Looking Glass

Over time, it has become apparent that Steve Jobs had an extraordinary ability to see customers' pain and to understand the customer experience and what about it could be improved. We mere mortals may not have such clairvoyance, or if we do, we may not be so confident in our own perceptions. So as a brief departure from the "What Would Steve Jobs Do?" theme, here are some things you can do or think about to enhance your view and your leadership of the customer experience:

- *"Carpet Time."* Innovation expert and author Nicholas Webb uses this term to describe a close, real-time observation of the customer experience. The term arose from his experiences watching his young children play, but he applies it in his practice, just watching a customer use a product from start to finish. Give a customer a product, in a brand-new box or not, and watch what she does with it. It's not a focus group—it's a start-to-finish observation, and you're doing it personally as a team leader.
- *Observe the mistakes of first movers.* Apple has typically not been the first to market in most of its categories. Personal computers, MP3 players, cell phones, and tablets all existed in some form before Apple perfected the category. Paying close attention to—and taking apart—first movers' mistakes is a great way to add customer value, and a great way to lead an organization. The Japanese did it with cars. Southwest did it with air travel. Don't be first—make it perfect instead.
- *See beneath the surface.* Steve Jobs intuitively grasped what was beneath the surface that was causing customer pain, and what could be done

about it. You and most of us might not be able to do that. So when you watch or talk to a customer, try to get to that "what's really bugging you about this experience?" question. You may not get an answer that you can use, but it's guaranteed that you won't get one if you don't ask.

PAIN PILL, PLEASE

There's a lot of pain out there, and there's a lot to gain if you take a close look. One of my pet peeves is the growing use of self-checkout scanners. Have you ever been held up in a line of four people waiting for someone to get a readable bar code for a 25-cent sprinkler part? It happens all the time. How many times have you had to call the attendant to resolve a problem (or prove that you're "of age" to buy that bottle of wine in a grocery)? How much customer pain have groceries and home improvement stores caused just to save a few $9-an-hour checkers? Think about it. Some groceries are, given their recent announcements that they are cutting back on self-checkout. Thank goodness.

Customer pain provided a good opportunity for CarMax, a rapidly growing retail-format purveyor of used cars. Its business model is, quite simply, to get away from the stereotypical used-car salesperson and used-car-buying process, and to add a bit of computer-aided management science to stocking and pricing decisions. This just goes to show that customer-driven innovations don't have to be high-tech.

And another pet peeve: the solar industry. Solar energy just hasn't really "crossed the chasm" to become mainstream. Is it the technology? I don't think so — I attribute it to customer pain. Customers must work with a dealer who marks everything up 100 percent and typically makes the whole installation sound more high-tech than it really is. It's a selling process, not a buying process. There's a big sales pitch and a huge dollar outlay. So, make modular solar panels available at Home Depot, so that you can add them as you need them, with a plug-in inverter with some basic installation instructions; if you do, a lot more people, including me, will go solar.

Fix the experience.

BE THE CUSTOMER

Finally, with the customer and the customer experience firmly in mind, the next step is simply to roll up your sleeves, take off your shoes, and put on the customers' shoes. See things through the customer's eyes. This is the third and final element of Steve Jobs's "passionate empathy" for the customer. Again, you as the leader need to do this, and not rely on others to do it for you.

The process can be done as a series of questions, something like this:

What Would I Want?

This sounds simple, but it amazes me how many leaders fail to consider what they would want in a product themselves, or as a typical customer. As the saying goes, there may be no "I" in "leadership," but there is an "I" in innovation: what would "I" want? If you've gotten the customer right by seeing her and seeing her experience, the "what would I want?" part should come pretty clearly.

Steve Jobs went a step further. Beyond just thinking about "What would I want?" from his own perspective, he encouraged his team members to play the same game. The designers and engineers and marketers and accountants and office assistants—everyone down the line—were encouraged to think about what they would want in a new product design or in a new product concept. Anything's possible, and if you want it and a lot of other people want it and it makes sense, why, let's build it.

Workers are more passionate about building things that they want, and that real customers want.

What Are the Deep Needs?

We've already covered this one. Does a customer just want a portable music player? Or does he want one that has superb sound and a superb sensory experience that's really easy to use, really looks cool, and is supported by 99-cent, one-click, easy-to-get songs? It's critical to think about the deep need, the *whole* need—don't just stop at the first or second product attribute that solves a customer issue.

What Would Surprise and Delight?

If you check into an average-priced hotel, you expect average features—a reasonably comfortable bed, clean towels, reasonable quiet from the outside street, an inside entry, pleasant décor. But what if you got a really nice breakfast in the morning? A free newspaper? Turn-down service?

True, these things are available at fancy hotels, and you'd probably expect them if you paid a fancy hotel's price. But what happens when you pay an average price? These "bonuses" will surprise and delight you.

Conversely, if enough "surprise and delight" factors are there consistently, you'll eventually be willing to pay a higher price. Customers respond well to—and pay more for—features, sensory experiences, and qualities that surprise and delight them. Simple surprises are the best—surprises that make the experience simpler, rather than more complicated, have the most impact. If you approach your business with a customer mindset, you'll always consider what might surprise or delight that customer. Remember, customers aren't likely to tell you, because they know only what you provide today. If they knew, it wouldn't be a surprise.

What would surprise and delight a customer about your product or service?

The Whole Product Should Be Positive

A customer-centered thinker realizes that the whole product is important—that is, the software, the services, the setup, the replacement path, the instructions, and so forth. It's not just about the box itself, as has been so plainly illustrated by Apple. No Apple product comes without a perfect OS, a perfect music service, and an app store that all work together to make the experience better.

Too many companies think only about the product, and may even go for a "surprise and delight" level of experience with the product. But they fail to think about the whole product—the total experience—in the same terms. They align themselves with the idea that the surrounding features and experiences should be a *nonnegative*, not a positive. If the sales process, the service experience, and the replacement experience are OK and not negatives, check the box; we're done.

Of course, a customer who loves your products may hate the rest of the experience and shy away. It's interesting how Toyota plays both sides of the fence on this one. It sells excellent cars under both the Toyota and the luxury Lexus nameplates. But the surrounding Toyota experience is terrible (obnoxious salespeople, boorish service), while Lexus customers get the white-glove treatment all the way. How much more would it cost Toyota to give its Toyota customers the Lexus experience? One wonders, but it sure as heck would help the image of the whole product.

Ask yourself: what would make *all* parts of the total customer experience exceed expectations? When you can answer that question, you have a 360-degree view of the customer, and you are ready to lead your organization forward.

SHOULD YOU TRY THIS YOURSELF?

Caveat leader. Do you want to be like Steve Jobs? Sure, but you need to appreciate the pitfalls. And there's one big elephant "pitfall" here that any aspiring Jobsian leader should consider.

Very simply, Steve had some extraordinary powers of customer intuition and customer vision. He didn't always get it right, but he got it right enough times in a big enough way to rightly be considered an expert on customer experience, at least in the businesses he operates in.

That was fine for him, and he had enough experience and enough capital to afford the risk that he might be wrong. That was good for him, but it's not hard to see how such a firm position of success could make one arrogant. I'm not saying that Steve Jobs was arrogant, but it is plainly possible for someone in his position who insists on approaching things his way to become a bit overconfident—and miss something.

We mortals can't do that. We mortals probably can't rely on our own raw intuition to the degree that he did. We probably need to study customers a bit more than he did, and we probably need outside help a bit more than he did. But we need to recognize the limitations of having others do it for us.

We might need training wheels for a while, but if we get the thought process right, and if we see the customer as the base and support of all things leadership in our worlds, the odds are that things will come out right.

We just need to protect ourselves in case we're wrong.

DEVELOPING YOUR OWN CUSTOMER CONNECTIVITY

An example of what Steve Jobs could probably do on the back of a napkin in a Cupertino, California, restaurant, but we can't without some thought, is the following "Quick 3" test offered by innovation consultant Nicholas Webb.

The "Quick 3" Test

- Can you quickly describe three things your customers like about your products?
- Can you quickly describe three things about your products that frustrate the heck out of your customers?
- Can you describe three experiences your customers have had with your products and have told you about recently?
- Are you getting three useful inputs or comments about your products each week?
- Have you been "in the field" at least three times in the past calendar quarter?

If you can answer these "threes" positively, you, and thus your organization, are on the right track.

VISION: THE GLUE CONNECTING THE CUSTOMER TO YOUR ORGANIZATION

Of course, if you become a customer expert, but you can't translate that expertise into a premise or a vision that your team can use, you won't get anywhere at producing market-beating, market-*defining* products. The message: leadership doesn't just stop with knowing the customer; that probably isn't a surprise. You need to expand that customer sense into a vision that the rest of the organization can use. That's the subject of Chapter 5.

JUST ANOTHER INNOVATION BOOK?

What Would Steve Jobs Do? may be starting to sound like a book on the topic of innovation. There are many such books. We can't talk about Steve Jobs without talking about innovation. Good leadership requires good innovation; without it, you aren't really leading, but rather fighting a rearguard action in the marketplace.

Good innovation is one of the major differences between leading and following, no matter what you're doing in the enterprise. So no, it's not a stand-alone topic. Innovation is a part of leadership, and customer knowledge is part of innovation. These principles apply whether you're making personal computers or potato chips.

WHAT WOULD STEVE JOBS DO?

- Be in charge of customer sense and of conveying that sense to the organization.
- Don't delegate or outsource that task.
- Don't assume that customers will know or tell you what they want.
- Think about customer pain and what causes it.
- Think about "deep needs."
- Consider the whole product.
- Consider what would surprise and delight your customer.
- Never stop adding to your customer knowledge.

CHAPTER 5

VISION

When Steve believes in something, the power of that vision can literally sweep aside any objections or problems. They just cease to exist.

—Trip Hawkins, former Apple VP
Strategy & Marketing

From the stage at Macworld 2007, on January 7, 2008, dressed in his trademark black turtleneck, faded jeans, and a pair of white sneakers, Steve Jobs, as he usually did, captured the day:

> This is a day I've been looking forward to for 2½ years. Every once in a while, a revolutionary product comes along and changes everything (and, first of all, one's very fortunate if you get to work on ONE of these in your career). Apple is very fortunate. It has been able to introduce a few of these into the world. In 1984, we introduced the Macintosh. It didn't just change Apple. It changed the whole computer industry [applause]. In 2001, we introduced the first iPod. And, it didn't just change the way we all listened to music. It changed the entire music industry. Well, today, we're introducing THREE revolutionary products of this class. The first one is a wide-screen iPod with touch controls [applause]. The second is a revolutionary mobile phone [applause], and the third is a breakthrough Internet communications device [applause].
> So, three things.

A wide-screen iPod with touch controls. A phone. And an Internet communications device.

An iPod. A phone. And an Internet communicator.
An iPod. A phone. And an Internet communicator.

Are you getting it? These are not three separate
devices. This is one device. And we are calling it
iPhone [steady applause].

Today, Apple is going to reinvent the phone.
And here it is (a picture of an iPod with a rotary
dial on it, laughter).

No, really, here it is [pulls one from his pocket
and holds it up for his audience].

We all know the rest of the story. The iPhone
changed the mobile phone industry.

That was 2007, and this is now. Jobs and his team did
it again. They synthesized the form and features of the
iPhone with the size and scope of the PC, and created
the iPad. The iPad is currently changing the entire personal computing industry.

What's next?

We don't know for sure. What we do know is that
time and time again, Steve Jobs and Apple changed the
game. Time and time again, they came up with the
"wow" solution that bundled technologies to leapfrog
the competition. Time and time again, they came up
with the "wow" solution that leapfrogged customer
expectations and created a new customer experience.

What we do know is that not only was Steve Jobs introducing a new product, but he was also articulating a *vision*. What does that mean? That's what this chapter is all about.

NOT INVENTED HERE— JUST MADE PERFECT

Did Apple invent the smartphone? The tablet? The MP3 player? Did Apple invent touchscreen technology or miniaturized storage or music downloads or the computer mouse or the graphical user interface?

As we all know, the answer is *no*. Apple didn't invent these things; they had all been on the market in some form, or well underway in a lab, before Steve Jobs and Apple did their thing.

Steve Jobs and Apple didn't invent these technologies. Instead, they perfected them. And in perfecting them, they combined them and packaged them beautifully. They combined and packaged and bundled them beautifully to meet or exceed a known customer desire—to listen to music, to make mobile calls, and to have access to the Internet.

They combined them beautifully to *create* customer needs—*future needs*, needs that we mortal customers didn't even know we had. Needs such as using computers to produce graphic newsletters and presentations, storing music libraries, and using simple "apps" to accomplish everyday tasks.

Steve Jobs and Apple put existing technologies to work. They put them together. They put them into a really cool, well-designed package—not only a beautiful physical plastic or aluminum or titanium case, but also bundled with the right services—to deliver a game-changing customer experience.

So how do you turn a bunch of stuff that's already out there into a game changer? What's the secret sauce that takes a solid customer sense, applies existing technologies to it, and sets the world on its ear?

It can all be summed up in one word: *vision*.

Vision is the ability to see the world ahead. Vision is the ability to see how ideas and technologies can be integrated to solve problems. Vision is the ability to see how ideas, technologies, and design can be redirected to create customer surprise and delight.

When it's done really well, vision is the ability to see how to make customers' lives better.

The Difference between Invention and Innovation

Did Apple invent the iPhone? Yes, in the purest sense, Apple created it. But really, the company *innovated* it. What do we mean?

Lots of people invent things. Patent offices worldwide are stuffed with new, original ideas for things, or ways to make things, or how to show things to people. But the number of patents that turn into game-changing products (or marketable products at all) is amazingly tiny.

For years, tech giants such as Hewlett-Packard and IBM bragged about how many patents had been issued for technologies they had developed in-house. They bragged in their colorful annual reports, and they bragged to the media. But how many of the 3,000 or more patents that these companies churned out each year ever got to market? Very few, if any. The last game-changing technology brought to market by HP was the inkjet printer, and that was back in 1984. The last IBM breakthrough doesn't even come to mind.

What's the difference? Both of these companies and many others spend big bucks on R&D. They have labs, and they have scientists and engineers hunkered down, usually in separate R&D facilities, to do basic research. They have lots of ideas, and they obviously know how to push them forward through the patent process. But they remain detached from the business and detached from the customer; there is no vision to accompany them.

In fact, this is the reason why Xerox doesn't rule the computer space today. It had the technology for the graphical user interface, the mouse, the laser printer, and basic networking at its Palo Alto PARC laboratories.

But there was no vision to guide these inventions to commercial success. Steve Jobs supplied the vision, and the rest is history.

Meanwhile, scores of individuals have good ideas, too. They may come up with them deliberately, or they may have them quite by accident. They may be by-products of other ideas. But do they ever get to market?

To get a patent, an idea must be original, must do something useful, and must be nonobvious. But does it have to sell? Does it have to sell profitably? Does it have to be marketable? Does it have to make lives better? Does it have to be noticed by the public? No, not at all.

That's the difference. Inventions, on their own, may be creative, but still not move the needle. Successful companies *innovate*. They create products; they integrate technologies into things that people *want to buy*. Really good innovations aren't just products; they are game-changing *solutions* to customer problems, like air conditioning, internal combustion engines, or even those colorful little candies that melt in your mouth, not in your hand—M&Ms.

I will define innovation in a way that probably would have made sense to Steve Jobs:

> Innovation is an invention with a customer and a marketable vision in mind.

To qualify as an innovation, an invention must be marketable. It must be noticeable, and it must be noticed. It must have true *value*; that is, it must be worth more to customers than they have to pay for it. And, importantly, it must be profitable to the company. The vast majority of inventions fail these tests. A few pass it, but not by enough to really move the needle. Can you remember the "what's new" about the latest PC or MP3 player or printer introduced by an Apple competitor?

And some innovations, like the iPod, the iPhone, and the iPad, have become synonymous with the term.

THE JAPANESE APPROACH
Success and Excellence, but No Vision

One can also look at the Japanese to understand the role that vision plays in innovation. As a rule, the Japanese understand customers, but they focus on mainstream customers, and they look for incremental improvements in the existing experience. They don't connect the customer experience with a vision for how it could change, only how it could be better within the confines and channels of the current product. They do a very good job at that, perhaps better than anyone else in the world.

But, with a few exceptions like the Sony Walkman, they don't define new product concepts or new markets. They stop short of being innovators. They fail to "think different"; their visions tend not to go very far ahead—like into the digital era with Walkman. Are they successful? Yes. But one can only imagine what they could do with a visionary leader like Steve Jobs in charge.

WHAT IS A VISIONARY?

Just as most Apple products introduced since Steve Jobs's 1997 return are considered to exemplify innovations, Steve Jobs himself was often considered to be synonymous with the term "visionary." I'll spend a few minutes on the term "visionary," as that is one of the best ways to capture what a vision is, why it's important, and how you can develop your vision skills as a leader—even if you aren't a visionary yourself.

The term "visionary" is thrown around rather loosely at times. Occasionally it comes up in a negative sense; in fact, some dictionary definitions focus on the notion of a "dreamer," someone who has visions or dreams that really aren't practical, let alone marketable. Someone with good ideas who can't get anything done.

I think we can discard that concept of a visionary, at least as it applies to Steve Jobs and Apple. Here are the best two definitions I found for the word "visionary."

- A person of strong and creative imaginative power and, often, the ability to inspire others (*Webster's New World College Dictionary*)
- A person with a clear, distinctive, and specific vision of the future, usually connected with advances in technology or social/political arrangements.

Okay, I got the second definition from Wikipedia. But whoever contributed that definition really captured the essence of what a visionary is and what he brings to the table, at least in today's tech-influenced world. I might add that the visionary can also *communicate* the vision to others in a way that inspires them, which circles back to the Webster definition. As we will see, effective visions—visions that can be acted upon—are clear, distinctive, and specific, and in Steve Jobs's world and in many commercial enterprises, they are connected with advances in technology.

CAN YOU BE A VISIONARY?

We've identified six elements of the Steve Jobs Leadership Model: Customer, Vision, Culture, Product, Message, and Brand.

You can get close to your customers, although it may take a while for you to really get a sense of them. You can build an innovation culture, and you can lead the way in building exciting products. You can deliver the message (although that might take some public speaking or even theatrical training), and you can build your own personal brand and the brand of the enterprise.

But can you become a visionary? Can you learn to be a visionary? Or is it a natural, inborn skill and talent? Indeed, becoming a true visionary is a tall order. Visionaries in the past, from Abraham Lincoln to Martin Luther King to Steve Jobs, typically weren't made; they were born with many of the innate thought patterns and skills that enabled them to see the future and communicate it to others.

But can you learn to think like a visionary—to see the world the way a visionary does? This might be possible, and the rest of this chapter engages with that idea. To start with, we need to identify some of the key parts of a vision.

WHAT IS A VISION?

I'll adapt the definition of a vision from the Wikipedia definition of a visionary:

A vision is a clear, distinctive, and specific view of human activities in the future and how those activities might be changed or made better.

It's worth a few minutes to explore this definition.

CLEAR, DISTINCTIVE, AND SPECIFIC

The genius of a good vision is that it is something distinctive and specific that is also clearly enough articulated that we can get behind it. It is something worth following.

For example, it might appear that slogans like "Achieve World Peace" or "Cure World Hunger" are visions. They are causes that we can all get behind, and they are clear—so far as they go. But are they distinctive and specific? Not really. If they offered a clue to how the world could really change to combat these problems and to become better, they might start to resemble a vision.

Steve Jobs's vision of integrating an iPod Touch, a phone, and an Internet communications device into one single package was more than a slogan. We don't have a specific vision statement to accompany the launch. But we can feel the vision of combining these devices, and adding the app store (which wasn't even mentioned), in a way that would have a considerable impact on how people used mobile devices, not only as phones, but as Internet and entertainment devices. It is clear, it is distinctive, and it is specific.

The "distinctive and specific" part is where so many visions fail.

Changed or Made Better

Taking a look again at the "Achieve World Peace" panaceas, the "changed or made better" part, ironically, is another place where they tend to fall apart. They don't have a clear, distinctive, and specific way to change the world or make it better. Jobs's vision for the iPhone obviously considered the economies and "coolness" of a single device, and if those economies didn't change the customer's world, the 500,000 apps available to run on the iPhone probably would.

Even the elegantly simple form factor and display screen were bound to make the smartphone user's world better. As Steve himself said, before the iPhone, "smartphones weren't very smart."

Ten Words or Fewer

The best visions are simple, and can be articulated in at most a sentence or two. Many of you are familiar with the "elevator speech," where you describe yourself, a product, or a project that you're working on clearly and succinctly in the time it takes to ride an elevator to a nearby floor.

An elevator speech may even be too long for a vision. Some people advocate articulating a vision in 10 words or fewer.

How about:

> An elegantly simple, smart iPod Touch, phone, and Internet connectivity in a single device.

That's 14 words. How about:

> An iPod Touch, phone, and Internet connectivity in a single device.

That's 11 words, close enough . . . and almost exactly what Steve said at Macworld 2007.

Or, paraphrasing another Jobs quote:

> Take state-of-the-art technology and make it easy for people.

As a customer, or as an employee, can you see how you could get your arms around such a core vision? Can you see how it would guide and direct your thoughts and actions as a member of this team?

THE TAGLINE MAY TELL

Sometimes you can find a company's vision right out in front in a corporate or product tagline. Used-car retailer CarMax uses "The Way Car Buying Ought to Be." Those seven words say a lot. They're clear, distinctive, and specific, and they suggest at least indirectly how the world is going to change. They tell both the customer and the employees what the company is all about, even though they don't go very far into the "how" of that promise.

A local employee benefits and insurance agency in my area uses "Employee Benefits. Made Simple. Done Right." That also goes a long way; again, both the customers and the employees have an idea of what the agency is all about. Anything that doesn't make employee benefits simpler or done right shouldn't be attempted.

While it isn't very specific, Apple's "Think Different" tagline says as much about the company and its direction as any 2 (or probably 10) other words possibly could.

DON'T CONFUSE VISION
WITH A MISSION

As most of you in the corporate world know, large organizations can get bogged down in layers of strategic planning (mission, goal, objectives, strategies, tactics), all laced with the latest jargon. These often-lengthy documents cover everything about who you are, what you do, and whom you do it for. Mission statements have their role, although they have a way of not getting much attention once they've been crafted, distributed, and filed in every employee's file cabinet.

As Carmine Gallo points out in his book *The Innovation Secrets of Steve Jobs*, "A mission statement describes what you make; a vision describes how you're going to make the world a better place."

As a follower, which would you rally around: a leader with a clear ten-word vision of how to make the world a better place, or a leader with a six-bullet-point mission statement?

DON'T CONFUSE VISION WITH PASSION

A visionary has passion, but vision and passion aren't the same thing. A passionate leader without a clear vision won't succeed; likewise, neither will a visionary leader without passion.

Passionate leaders without a vision will often confuse the troops or put a higher level of energy and stress on the organization. That organization will flounder around with frequent starts and stops and strategy changes, and will eventually burn out. Visionary leaders without passion will have a hard time keeping their troops engaged, and some may question the veracity or credibility of the vision in the first place if the leader doesn't seem to be excited about it.

Vision and passion go together. A leader who has a good vision and is passionate about it will get further with subordinates. Abraham Lincoln showed that with his unwavering focus on preserving the Union and his undivided passion for doing so. Steve Jobs exuded passion to the absolute max in his creation of a team, in his messages to the team, in his attention to the details of the project, and in his theatrical product launches. Nobody could question his passion, and thus, nobody could question his vision. The passion made the vision stronger.

As a leader, you need to realize that passion and vision must be in balance; too much passion without enough vision is confusing and stressful; too much vision without passion can be bland and alienating.

It's All about Synthesis

More often than not, a vision is a synthesis of ideas or products or technologies around a specific customer need or idea. For those of us who don't develop visions naturally, or at least as naturally as Steve Jobs did, here are a few patterns you can follow to build or enhance a vision:

- *Visions combine things.* Ideas, products, and technologies are "mushed" together to arrive at an epiphany solution. The iPod Touch, a phone, and an Internet communications device became the iPhone. Earlier on, a small disk drive, a new battery, FireWire, and iTunes turned into the iPod. Still earlier, a graphical user interface, a one-piece cabinet, and a 3.5-inch floppy drive became the Macintosh.

- *Visions connect things.* Visionaries can apply or "cross" existing concepts or technologies across new platforms. The modern "big-box" retail format was crossed with the traditional lumberyard to come up with Home Depot, and was crossed with the used-car business to create CarMax. The love of coffee and an Italian ambience were crossed with the decline of alcohol and the corner bar to create the Starbucks coffee vision. The iPad could be loosely described as a cross between a PC and an iPhone.

- *Visions apply the new to the old.* This is similar to the connect idea, except that it specifically involves new technologies. Digital technology and miniaturization can be applied to modernize a traditional music (or book) library. Microwave technology, developed for defense applications, can be used to cook food (that originally seemed to be a bigger vision than it actually turned out to be, because microwaves don't cook all foods well). Many a vision for how to apply the Internet to almost anything came forth during the dot-com boom—but just because someone has a vision doesn't mean it's right!

- *Visions create value propositions.* Customers are usually willing to trade off something to get something better, and value proposition–centered visions capitalize on this. Southwest had a clear vision that customers would accept no meals in flight, no first class, no assigned seats, and no interline baggage in return for cheap fares. CarMax figured that people would pay a somewhat higher price to get a haggle-free and trustworthy car buying experience. Starbucks figured that people would pay $3.45 for a latte to get an intellectually stimulating third place. Apple figured that people would pay 99 cents for songs to get a reliable download and copyright peace of mind.

If you know your customers and know your business, you should be able to build a vision around one or more of these patterns.

WHAT WOULD STEVE JOBS DO?

Few things were more important to Steve Jobs and the Apple organization than vision. While Steve was connected enough with his business to get into the details of product design (and often did), his real contribution was the vision and the passion necessary to conceive, develop, and market the right products, over and over. Steve used his deep customer sense, his broad worldview, and his understanding of technology to formulate some "amazingly great" visions. These visions fueled— and were fueled by—the innovation culture that supported them. Together, the visions and the culture led to the development of amazing products. The building and nurturing of the innovation culture is the subject of the next chapter. In the meantime, here's what Steve would have done—and you should, too—concerning vision:

- *Stay focused on the customer.* Always. Otherwise, the vision will lead you astray.
- *Take inventory of what's out there.* Constantly monitor the competition to see who's doing what, how customers respond to it, and what gaps are left to be filled.

- *Think how things can combine and evolve.* Think of a future, and how you can combine what exists today or in the near future to deliver it.

- *Articulate the idea.* It isn't a good idea until it is clear, distinctive, and specific. Work on that. A clear and compelling vision, as Hawkins says, will sweep objections away.

- *Try it out on outsiders.* Of course, you want your organization's response and feedback on a vision. But if your vision makes sense to your next-door neighbor, your mother-in-law, and your dog, you're even more on the right track.

- *Keep it in front of the organization.* Keep everyone in your group in constant touch with what you're thinking and what you're seeing.

- *Always be willing to adapt or refine the vision.* Never assume that your vision is perfect, or that the world won't change. Arrogance is a vision's worst enemy.

CHAPTER 6

CULTURE

Real artists ship.

—*Steve Jobs, Macintosh team off-site,*
January 1983

Time magazine, obviously taken with the success of Apple and the evolution of the iPod, did an extensive front-page cover story and interview with Steve Jobs in September 2005, a rare media appearance during this period.

Steve told *Time* a story that he's told before: "The Parable of the Concept Car." It goes like this:

> "Here's what you find at a lot of companies," he says, kicking back in a conference room at Apple's gleaming white Silicon Valley headquarters, which looks something like a cross between an Ivy League university and an iPod. "You know how you see a show car, and it's really cool, and then four years later you see the production car, and it sucks? And you go, 'What happened? They had it! They had it in the palm of their hands! They grabbed defeat from the jaws of victory!'
>
> "What happened was, the designers came up with this really great idea. Then they take it to the engineers, and the engineers go, 'Nah, we can't do that. That's impossible.' And so it gets a lot worse. Then they take it to the manufacturing people, and they go, 'We can't build that!' And it gets a lot worse."
>
> (Full article: http://www.time.com/time/ magazine/article/0,9171,1118384,00.html)

This little story goes miles toward explaining perhaps the most important element of leading a business: the creation and nourishment of an innovation culture. Steve gave his view of why innovation doesn't happen in a typical culture, which, of course, we can carefully turn around to arrive at what really *does* work in a Steve Jobs organization.

THE CULTURE OF CAN DO

"Culture" describes the work environment and personality of an organization. It is a "collection of values and norms that are shared by people and groups" that guides how these people and groups interact with one another and with outsiders. Some cultural norms are conscious and tangible, written down and drilled into workers' heads. Others are quite subconscious and intangible, originating from the greater vision, purpose, and history of an organization.

Culture describes what an organization will do, how it will behave, and how it will respond to marketplace requirements. As a brand is to a product, a culture is a predictable pattern of activities, attitudes, and interactions that defines how something gets done. Culture can also dictate what an organization *won't* do, such as bogging down innovation and response to the marketplace with red tape and excessive risk management.

Culture goes a long way toward explaining the unique qualities of the Steve Jobs–led Apple organization that have led it to prosper and put their stamp on corporate history. Quite obviously, the Apple culture is one of innovation, a fertile ground for vision "seeds" to germinate into healthy game-changing products. What is an "innovation culture"? I'll offer a simple definition, which again I think would have passed muster with Steve Jobs:

> An innovation culture is a work environment that enhances, rather than impedes, the delivery of visionary products to the market.

VISION AND CULTURE—A HAPPY COUPLE

Vision and culture go together. A company with an innovation culture is easily driven by an innovative vision; a company with an innovative vision is more likely to display an innovation culture. If you lack a solid innovation culture, even the best customer sense and vision for the future will fail to produce game-changing products. When combined, a vision and a strong innovation culture work together to bridge the gap between the customer and the product.

If the vision and the culture are not both in place and in balance, strange things can happen. A strong innovation culture with no vision will be directionless; it may hit a winner by accident, but that's unlikely. A strong vision without a strong innovation culture will fail, as the visionary will constantly be shot down by process and the "organizational antibodies," the assortment of players who see no gain from taking risk and departing from what's already been done.

A good innovation culture is a culture of "can do." It is a culture that enthusiastically embraces the vision. It is a culture that looks for ways to do something rather than reasons not to do something. It is a team that consistently produces amazing results without excessive structure, process, or coercion. The absence of barriers and bureaucracy allows good ideas to be developed rather than taken apart every step of the way. It is holistic—that is, it pervades the organization.

It is a positive, not a negative, culture.

DO WE REALLY INNOVATE?

In their annual reports, statements to the media, and financial presentations, many companies crow about having an "innovation culture" or being "innovation driven" or doing "innovation for tomorrow." But what do they really mean? Does the IBM or HP patent mill represent an innovation culture? Is a company that spends 10 percent of its revenues on R&D innovation driven? Not necessarily. Does a company with a big R&D lab, such as Alcatel-Lucent (Bell Labs), have an innovation culture? Not necessarily. Does a company that makes "Invent" its tagline, as HP did, have an innovation culture? Probably not.

One word, or a couple of words, does not make for an innovation culture. Innovation must happen naturally as part of the culture throughout the company to count.

An Organizational Vision—in Three Words

More than anything else, all Steve Jobs's organizations, from Apple to NeXT to Pixar, have lived these three words: "Real artists ship." The three words say a lot. First, Steve is calling his team a team of artists. He recognizes the creative and multidisciplinary talents of his team members. But to be relevant, or real, they must produce products that delight customers, and that ultimately sell.

In these three words lies the big difference between a Steve Jobs organization and most others. Most organizations are so focused on the "ship" part that they neglect the creativity and synthesis of the vision. At the same time, artists can be so driven by the creative, new, and avant garde that they fail to produce anything of value, that is, anything that will appeal to the customer and command a premium price.

Steve Jobs connected the two ideas like no leader in history. But it went beyond that: with unstoppable evangelism, passion, and support, Steve Jobs added a certain magic to an organization.

It quickly became a well-organized, functional group of artists that—yes indeed—shipped.

What Is a Culture Made Of?

Culture, like vision, has a certain intangible quality that's hard to identify. Culture works—or doesn't work—to produce innovations, but every corporate culture is slightly different. It's a bit like pornography: a good culture defies precise definition, but you know it when you see it.

Culture comes from leadership. Leaders select the team, set the vision and tone, and should determine or heavily influence how the team will work together to produce results. Culture is innate and continuous; it is not something that starts and stops when a team develops a product.

Leaders face at least four primary duties to make and maintain a culture of innovation and excellence:

- Selecting the team
- Organizing the team

- Sharing the passion
- Keeping the focus

We'll cover each of these in turn.

"IT'S MORE FUN TO BE A PIRATE THAN TO JOIN THE NAVY"

This quote, made back in the days of the original Mac development team, says a lot about how Steve viewed people and selected them for teams. It also speaks to the kind of team and team behavior he admired. To build a team, all organizations seek the best and the brightest people, particularly for their innovation and new product development organizations—that's not what's in question here. By seeking out the pirates, Steve took the idea a big step further.

Why pirates?

A pirate can function without a bureaucracy. Pirates support one another and support their leader in the accomplishment of a goal. A pirate can stay creative and on task in a difficult or hostile environment. A pirate can act independently and take intelligent risks, but always within the scope of the greater vision and the needs of the greater team.

Pirates are more likely to embrace change and challenge convention. "Being aggressive, egocentric, or antisocial makes it easier to ponder ideas in solitude or challenge convention," says Dean Keith Simonton, a University of California psychology professor and an expert on creativity. "Meanwhile, resistance to change or a willingness to give up easily can derail new initiatives."

So Steve's message was: if you're bright, but you prefer the size and structure and traditions of the navy, go join IBM. If you're bright and think different and are willing to go for it as part of a special, unified, and unconventional team, become a pirate.

Pirates with Passion

Steve looked for the pirate in all his team members. But it wasn't enough just to be brilliant, and it wasn't enough just to think different. Steve's pirates had to have the passion, the drive, and the shared vision to want to delight the customer with a perfect, game-changing product. Steve was constantly worried that as Apple grew, it would become like other big companies: tied up in bureaucracy, with a hundred reasons why something couldn't be done. Pirates with passion would not let this happen. In keeping with this idea, Steve wanted his pirates not only for the product development organizations, but also for routine business functions like accounting and even his administrative assistants.

As Steve told *Fortune* editor Betsy Morris in 2008: "When I hire somebody really senior, competence is the ante. They have to be really smart. But the real issue for me is, Are they going to fall in love with Apple? Because if they fall in love with Apple, everything else will take care of itself. They'll want to do what's best for Apple, not what's best for them, what's best for Steve, or anybody else."

WELL-TRAVELED PIRATES

Steve Jobs placed a lot of value on having a diverse organization, and on choosing individuals with diverse backgrounds and sets of experiences, like his own. As described in Chapter 1, Steve never finished college—not even his first year. But he was able to synthesize his own interests and experiences, from electronics hacking to Zen Buddhism to calligraphy, add three heaping scoops of passion, and become what he became. He felt that others should do the same.

When selecting team members, Steve looked for the same breadth of background and experiences. A good technologist is a good technologist, but one with interests in philosophy, the arts, literature, and such really moved the needle. He also liked entrepreneurship and signs of success at other endeavors. People who show the ability to get things done in other fields, to synthesize their experiences, and to take a broader view of the human experience are more likely to be the pirates that Steve was searching out. In a March 2011 iPad event, Steve told us: "It's in Apple's DNA that technology alone is not enough. That it's technology married with liberal arts, married with the humanities, that yields us the result that makes our hearts sing."

You Can Find a Pirate Anywhere

Not surprisingly, as Steve Jobs looked for people with diverse backgrounds, he would look everywhere. He was known to recruit the friends and acquaintances of his existing team members, feeling that they were most likely to fit with the team and share many of the same values. Apple doesn't do a lot of outbound recruiting— these days it doesn't have to, but even in the old days, people were just as likely to be found through happenstance and connections as through formal recruiting efforts. Even John Sculley was brought to Steve's attention by two of Steve's early Stanford recruits.

Once a contact was made with a prospective pirate, the interview was likely to depart from the norm. It wasn't your typical engineering interview. Diverse, seemingly off-task questions often bring diverse answers, and Steve was known to rely not so much on what people said as on how they said it, and on the meta-data that came in around the actual answer. Again, from the *Fortune*

interview: "Recruiting is hard. It's just finding the nee-
dles in the haystack. We do it ourselves and we spend a
lot of time at it. I've participated in the hiring of maybe
5,000-plus people in my life. So I take it very seriously.
You can't know enough in a one-hour interview. So, in
the end, it's ultimately based on your gut. How do I feel
about this person? What are they like when they're chal-
lenged? Why are they here? I ask everybody that: 'Why
are you here?' The answers themselves are not what you're
looking for. It's the meta-data."

So, in Steve's book—recruit a team of diverse, well-
traveled, and highly skilled pirates, and they'll follow you
anywhere.

"THE SYSTEM IS THAT THERE IS NO SYSTEM"

In October 2004, Steve did a revealing interview for an
article in *BusinessWeek* called "The Seeds of Apple's
Innovation." When asked: "How do you systematize
innovation?" he responded with the quote in the head-
ing. He went on to say, "That doesn't mean we don't
have processes. Apple is a very disciplined company, and
we have great processes. But that's not what it's about."

And then: "But innovation comes from people meeting
up in the hallways or calling each other at 10:30 at night
with a new idea, or because they realized something that

shoots holes in how we've been thinking about a problem. It's ad hoc meetings of six people called by someone who thinks he has figured out the coolest new thing ever and who wants to know what other people think of his idea."

The quote speaks volumes for what goes on inside Apple.

Steve Jobs hated bureaucracy. He hated the layers of management, the structure, the manuals, the procedures, the risk-management techniques that tend to grow and eventually choke typical large organizations. Put simply, he wanted the focus to be on customer and product, not process.

No Internal Focus, Please . . .

Process focus typically arises when organizations grow in size. When they grow, each team member gets a relatively smaller role or task in a greater or larger whole. When people are involved in increasingly smaller fractions of a project or a program, the tendency is to introduce formal processes to enable them to communicate and to make sure that each team member continues to contribute her piece on schedule.

Layers of management, cumbersome communication processes, checkpoint meetings, and various other forms of overhead begin to infiltrate the organization. Pretty soon, team members spend more time preparing for—

and focusing on—these internal processes and process delegates than they do on the customer or on anything else that is happening outside the business. Like the proverbial auto assembly-line worker, they lose the vision of the car and focus on the bolt that needs to be added, over and over.

The organization itself starts to serve its own interests rather than the needs of the customer. Everything happens to achieve some internal objective or meet some internal protocol. Even the R&D team begins to worry about achieving its objective to create patents, not to create exciting experiences for customers.

Steve Jobs was determined not to let this happen in his organizations. Early on, the tentacles of bureaucracy began to settle in on the Apple II team, with 4,000 employees, under John Sculley. Jobs's way out—and a better example—was the 100-person Macintosh team. But ultimately the forces of bureaucracy won out, almost nixing the 1984 Super Bowl commercial as well, as the organization became more about serving itself and less about changing the world.

NO "ONE AND NINE," PLEASE . . .

If you work for a large organization, you've probably experienced it. I know I have. When there are nine people doing the planning, checking the work, and shuffling the paper for every one person who is actually working on the customer solution, the tentacles of bureaucracy have finally choked the beast. When you work to create excellence, and people line up to scrutinize your procurement decisions, modify your office environment, prepare reports, and market your efforts to other silos *inside* the organization, you've probably crossed over to the dark side. It's easier to tear something apart than to create it, and individuals in these layers make careers out of tearing things apart.

As Nick Webb asks in *The Innovation Playbook*: "Does the process serve innovation? Or does Innovation serve the process?"

No Silos, Please

Steve Jobs was well known for preferring holistic end-to-end product and team thinking. He led the design of whole products—hardware and software, core product and accessories, all together—feeling that any time you leave pieces of the product to another company or organization, something will be left out. He thus shunned allowing the Microsoft OS to be used on other manufacturers' hardware models as an invitation to trouble, if not a formula that produced less successful products.

When it came to teams, Steve felt the same way. When projects are transferred from one organizational silo to another, problems are inevitable. Each silo takes care of its own needs and views the product in its own context, losing sight of the customer solution that was envisioned in the first place. Famously, Microsoft didn't get its tablet computing platform off the ground, even though Bill Gates himself predicted way back in 2001 that the tablet would overtake the PC—in part because the manager of the Microsoft Office software program didn't believe in tablets and didn't want to create a tablet version of Office.

How siloed is this? From one of the world's premier technology companies? Needless to say, it surprised a lot of people in the industry, but it goes a long way to illustrate Microsoft's lack of an innovation culture—a big reason that the company is struggling today to replicate its past PC software successes.

In many companies, the R&D organization, entrenched in its separated lab facilities off in the middle of corporate nowhere, is even treated as a silo itself. Siloed organizations and siloed thinking have clearly hurt other big companies—General Motors and HP are obvious examples in the marketplace, and many more would come to light if you looked inside their four walls.

As an alternative, Steve preferred small, holistic, empowered teams. In an effort to avoid bureaucracy and stay on task, the Macintosh team allegedly never exceeded 100 people. Sure, there was structure within the team; Steve didn't manage them all individually. But he kept it small and simple and worked directly with any team member as needed to keep things on track— and trusted that a lot would happen without his direct guidance.

Having a clear vision is one of the biggest keys to keeping a small team on track and to having a small team in the first place. Big teams arise in part where people aren't sure of or don't share the vision, so that team members and managers need to hash out stuff along the way. The skills, self-motivation, and open-mindedness of team members provide a lot of the self-governance that the team needs, but it starts to not work if the team is too big or the vision is unclear.

As Steve put it himself: "Put together small teams of great people and set them to build their dreams."

It's Okay to Take a Chance

As organizations grow, they tend to take fewer risks. Why? Because individuals are farther away from the customer and the vision, and as a result, they don't see and feel the benefits and rewards of delighting the customer. Meanwhile, what they *do* see is the risk of doing something that goes badly or fails—and the risk of losing their jobs in the process. So what do they do? They err on the side of avoiding failure.

Organizations naturally grow and evolve this way. Individuals and groups start working to cover their backsides instead of taking risks to move the company forward and exceed expectations. It becomes a modus operandi. Soon the organization as a whole is focusing on the last failure and trying to avoid it, rather than on the last success. Nick Webb calls that "failure referencing"—the tendency to default to failure as what will probably happen to a new idea because that's what happened last time.

Steve didn't let failure, or failure referencing, get in the way. He talked about success, and he energized the team to believe that an idea was a success until proven otherwise—"success referencing." People who brought new ideas or took risks weren't punished as long as they had a rationale for what they did. What Steve really hated was not the risk takers but the "bozos" who slowed things down without reason or who were in conflict with the vision.

University of California's Dr. Simonton chimes in on this, too: "Freedom to take risks, do a variety of assignments, and work on multiple projects at once can spark flexible thinking," while "pressure to play it safe or close off alternative perspectives can shut down creativity."

THAT DOESN'T MEAN YOU DON'T SAY NO

Not everything flies at Apple; in fact, a lot of things don't. Steve told *BusinessWeek* in October 2004 that success "comes from saying no to 1,000 things to make sure we don't get on the wrong track or try to do too much. We're always thinking about new markets we could enter, but it's only by saying no that you can concentrate on the things that are really important."

What does this mean? Ideas should be killed because they don't match the vision, not because they're risky.

"THE ONLY WAY TO DO GREAT WORK IS TO LOVE WHAT YOU DO"

Apple's can-do culture would have never come to exist without a healthy dose of passion. Today, many people in the business and academic worlds study the forces that get people to do things, and they lump these forces into the general category of "motivation." The conventional wisdom is: if you provide clear direction and a decent work environment and put the right financial and career rewards at the end of the tunnel, your team will be motivated to execute the work and move on to the next thing.

This idea of motivation jumps into hyperspace mode when it comes to Apple. From the beginning, Steve Jobs was passionate about "putting a dent in the universe"; that passion bubbled up in Steve's external presentations and in his internal communications and behaviors. It trickled down to every employee in the organization— and has done so throughout Apple's history. Passion directed in the right direction—that is, toward the vision—is indispensable, yet it is so hard to achieve. How did Steve Jobs do it?

The Chance to Do Something Special

Really smart, creative, broad-minded people like to work on really smart, creative, broad-minded things. This is where the vision and the track record for game-changing products enter the picture. People come into the organization with the idea that they can change the world, that they can be an important part of something that is big, complete, and special. They can be part of something really cool selling to millions of people worldwide that they, themselves, not a bunch of outsiders or consultants, have everything to do with. At Dell or HP, even if you have an important role in designing the latest PC, you know that the majority of the customer experience is still controlled by Microsoft. How easy is it to get passionate about that?

Steve described it this way to *BusinessWeek* in 2004 when he was asked why people wanted to work at Apple: "The reason is, is because you can't do what you can do at Apple anywhere else. The engineering is long gone in most PC companies. In the consumer electronics companies, they don't understand the software parts of it. And so you really can't make the products that you can make at Apple anywhere else right now. Apple's the only company that has everything under one roof."

You can see a chicken-and-egg question in this. The chance to do something special lures in the best and most creative minds. And it takes the best, most creative minds in a supportive environment to do something special. Which came first? It started with Steve Jobs and Steve Wozniak; great minds were drawn their way, and a few great products were created. It has been an upward spiral ever since. Great minds spawn great visions, which in turn create great products; more great minds jump onboard, and the upward spiral proceeds.

Again, for *BusinessWeek*, when asked about what drives Apple employees, Steve commented: "We don't get a chance to do that many things, and everyone should be really excellent. Because this is our life. Life is brief, and then you die, you know? So this is what we've chosen to do with our life. We could be sitting in a monastery somewhere in Japan. We could be out sailing. Some of the [executive team] could be playing golf. They could be running other companies. And we've all chosen to do this with our lives. So it better be damn good. It better be worth it. And we think it is."

Of course, we see many great minds in today's business world. But if they don't have great visions, and if they approach things in a "what's in it for me" manner, that will also trickle down to their teams. They will attract only people with a "what's in it for me" mentality to the team. When "what's in it for me" is the culture, people become disengaged from their work, and mediocrity—or worse—is the natural result.

GREAT EXPECTATIONS

Somewhere over the horizon beyond plain-vanilla motivation lies *inspiration*. Inspiration happens when people actually feel something, when they are *moved* by the potential result. You may be motivated to mow the lawn and trim the weeds, because if you don't, they'll take over your yard, and by the way, you'll save $50 on a landscaping service. But you may also be *inspired* by the idea of having the nicest-looking yard on the block, or even more by a possible *Sunset* magazine article. Who knows?

A greater expectation, or a "noble purpose," as author Carmine Gallo describes it, engenders greater commitment, harder work, and more creativity. People become more involved. Gallo goes on to note the Pygmalion effect, a psychological phenomenon where "the greater the expectation that is placed on people, the better they perform." Have you felt this when people at work were really counting on you to pull something together? As a parent or in your romantic life? In sports? Talented people tend to rise to the occasion; the right mix of people with the right vision in mind typically rises to this. The result: not only do they meet tough expectations, but they typically beat them.

In today's corporate world, what's more likely to happen is a "negative Pygmalion"—if you don't do X, here are the consequences. Yes, it's a high expectation, but it doesn't involve vision, brilliance, or game-changing results. It's another form of failure referencing. You may be motivated, but you won't be inspired.

Inspiration leads to the kinds of sacrifices and perseverance necessary to get things done; mere motivation does not. That kind of inspiration must come from the top.

KEEPING THE FOCUS

So did Steve Jobs merely set the vision, lead a few meetings, set the ball rolling, and go hang out at a bunch of Wall Street analyst presentations or go home awaiting the next Macworld or other product announcement forum? Not at all; he was deeply involved at almost every level with almost every critical project. And he was just as deeply involved in making his people feel important, eager to beat expectations, and ready to work on the next product. Perpetual inspiration was a key component of Steve's leadership style.

FINGER ON THE PULSE

Steve was an active practitioner of "managing by wandering around," or MBWA, a phrase popularized by Bill Hewlett and Dave Packard of HP. Steve attended checkpoint meetings, design reviews, and other meetings related to product development. Team members knew that at any time he might show up at their desks to find out what was happening. When *BusinessWeek* interviewed him in 2004, he estimated that he left half the day-to-day management to his executive team so that he could "spend half [his] time on the new stuff."

Steve's behavior in meetings and in these individual encounters was described by some as being petulant, harsh, and even boorish at times. He would ask a few tough questions and might get impatient, but according to most accounts, the tone settled into a normal conversation once he realized that what people were doing was on track with the vision and with the product development path.

By keeping his fingers on the pulse this way, he was doing three things. One, he was staying informed about the nuts and bolts of a project so that he could ask better questions and make more astute observations at the next meeting—or at the next desk. Two, he was rekindling the inspiration, reminding each employee how important *her* contribution was. Three, he was setting a good example, letting people know that just because he was a world-renowned billionaire, he was not above what they were doing. According to former VP and right-hand man Jay Elliot, "People become very connected to what they are doing—creating the product—because they know how connected their leader is."

Steve told *BusinessWeek* in 2004: "We've got 25,000 people at Apple. About 10,000 of them are in the stores. And my job is to work with sort of the top 100 people, that's what I do. That doesn't mean they're all vice presidents. Some of them are just key individual contributors. So when a good idea comes, you know, part of my job is to move it around, just see what different people think, get people talking about it, argue with people about it, get ideas moving among that group of 100 people, get different people together to explore different aspects of it quietly, and, you know—just explore things."

For Steve Jobs, being everywhere and hands-on was about product and company, not about power. With Steve Jobs, hands-on could be an exhilarating experience.

Letting 'Em Know You Appreciate It

From the early days, Steve Jobs learned to recognize and share success with his employees. Early accounts describe personal recognition of employees for every success delivered, including personally delivering bonuses, free products, and free medals and T-shirts commemorating a product launch to people's desks. Travelers got to travel first class, and everyone got to share in a pleasant work environment with refrigerators stocked with drinks, usually Odwalla juices, a Jobs favorite.

Back in the Mac days, he allowed each designer to personally sign a placard that was reproduced and placed inside each Mac case (most buyers never saw it, but it meant a lot to the team). Celebrations were frequent and notable, not just at launch but at every milestone, with pizza parties in the office and "team-building" off-sites in the Carmel/Monterey, California area. Free products are still the norm, with every employee receiving an iPhone on that product's launch. Employees have always received products either free or deeply discounted, which simultaneously boosts morale and gets the product out there for outsiders to see. In today's world of gadgets, it's surprising how rarely this happens.

Rewards are nice, but just as important is letting everyone know how important *his* contribution is. Steve was a master at that craft. While he could "take away" pretty quickly if you weren't with the program, he could also "give" with great generosity and praise. He was nothing if not empathetic. Messages were delivered in such a way as to both reward and recognize people and fire them up for the next accomplishment.

WHAT WOULD STEVE JOBS DO?

An interview with *Fortune* magazine in 1998 gave a nice summary of the Steve Jobs culture and how it differed from the rest: "Innovation has nothing to do with how many R&D dollars you have. When Apple came up with the Mac, IBM was spending at least 100 times more on R&D. It's not about money. It's about the people you have, how you're led, and how much you get it."

Here are a few strategies for building a Steve Jobs culture:

- *Create an exciting vision.* It is hard to create an innovation culture without one. Do something special.
- *Find pirates.* But not just any pirates—pirates with passion.

- *Seek diversity of experience.* Recognize that diversity expands the view of the human experience. Diversity expands the view of how it can be moved forward.
- *Look at the résumé; then look beyond the résumé.* Look at the meta-data. Look for signs of success and forward-thinking creativity.
- *Keep the organization simple.* Keep it as holistic as possible. No self-serving bureaucracies. The process should support innovation, not the other way around.
- *Let people take intelligent risks.* Success reference; don't failure reference.
- *Avoid siloed organizations and avoid siloed thinking.*
- *Be the vision and be the product.* Live it every day.
- *Don't be afraid to expect too much.* If the vision is right, it will energize people.
- *Stay close to your team.* Empathize. Mingle. Pat people on the back. Be honest. Keep it about the product and the customer, not about money and power.
- *Always set an excellent example.*

CHAPTER 7

PRODUCT

We used to dream about this stuff. Now
we get to build it. It's pretty great.

Steve Jobs, Worldwide Developer
Conference, 2004

At Apple's Worldwide Developer Conference in 2010, Steve Jobs took the stage again:

We're introducing iPhone 4—the fourth-generation iPhone. Now . . . this is really hot. And there are over 100 new features, and we don't have time to cover them today, so I get to cover eight of them with you, eight new features of the iPhone 4. The first one: an all new design. Now . . . stop me if you've already seen this [laughter in reference to previous alleged design leaks] . . . believe me, you ain't seen it. You've got to see this thing in person; it is one of the most beautiful designs you've ever seen. This is beyond a doubt the most precise thing, one of the most beautiful things we've ever made. Glass on the front and the rear and stainless steel running around, and the precision with which this is made is beyond any consumer product we've ever seen. It's closest kin is like a beautiful old Leica camera. It's unheard of in consumer products today . . . just gorgeous . . . and it's really thin . . . this is the new iPhone 4 [applause].

Steve went on for another two minutes to describe the new features, including the two-part stainless steel case that doubles as a dual-purpose antenna "built into

the structure of the phone; it's never been done before . . .
it's really cool engineering." He finished, "I don't think
there's another consumer product like this . . . when you
hold this in your hands . . . it's unbelievable."

This presentation, like most of Steve's presentations,
clearly showed his deep involvement with and knowledge of the product. How many other CEOs have you
seen publicly hold up or sit in or drive or experience
one of their company's products? I'm continually
amazed that, with a few exceptions like Chrysler's Lee
Iacocca and Herb Kelleher of Southwest Airlines, you
almost never see a CEO in the same picture as one of
the company's products, let alone holding it and
demonstrating it and telling everyone how it works as
lovingly as Steve did.

Steve Jobs sent a clear and undeniable message: he
cared.

COOL AIR AT THE SUMMIT

In Steve Jobs's world, Product is the culminating climax
and Holy Grail of the leadership chain, which starts way
back at Customer. We have two more chapters in this
book, Message and Brand, which, of course, add icing to
the cake. But make no mistake: Apple's mission and
Steve's mission stand at the peak of the mountain when
an excellent game-changing product—a *whole* prod-

uct—finds its way into the marketplace and into a customer's hands.

What Would Steve Jobs Do? is not a product design manual, so we won't go into much detail about product design and the history of Apple product designs here. Instead, in this chapter, we will explore the importance of product and the role of product in the greater leadership process.

I have identified three standout characteristics of product, which are tied closely to Steve's style of leadership. As a leader of your own organization, you can take cues from Steve's attitude and his emphasis on these three attributes of a product. Beyond the products themselves, these attributes also define how Steve saw the world, and many of these principles were applied not only to products, but to the corporation as a whole:

- Platform, not product
- Elegant simplicity
- The cool factor

You could sum this up in a three-word guide to product design and leadership: complete, simple, and cool.

"It's Not a Phone, It's a Platform"

Think about your last experience buying a technology product (other than an Apple). A laptop PC, for example. You may have searched a manufacturer's website to learn about it. There was the same old Web-page format, the same "speeds and feeds" statistics, nothing special; now you need to find a place to buy it. Suppose that is a conventional electronics retailer. You walk in. You hear the noise of a thousand unrelated electronics products blaring away in the background. You walk into the PC area. You stand around for a while. Finally a 20-year-old in a blue smock with a ring in his nose asks you if you need any help. You ask a few questions, get a few standard answers, and buy the machine after standing in line behind someone who was buying a new vacuum cleaner.

You go home to set up your new laptop. You turn it on, and it works. But now Microsoft takes over the experience. You set up Windows and register. You're good for now, but for all intents and purposes, you're a Microsoft customer. The pattern continues. You want music? You load iTunes or Rhapsody or some such. You want other programs to run on your new machine? Back to shopping mode. Then there are time-consuming software installations and dealing with those vendors.

Then something happens to the machine, and the screen goes dark. You call the 800 number, and an agent 12 times zones away reads through a long list of prefabricated questions. Your machine doesn't work. Now you're at the mercy of your electronics store or returning your product to the manufacturer. Are you dealing directly with the company that made the software? No. Are you dealing with the company that made the product? Maybe or maybe not—depending on how much of its service the company has outsourced.

You get the idea. You don't have an integrated product that was designed as a whole product. And you don't have an integrated experience that was designed as a whole customer experience.

A PRODUCT, OR A BUNDLE?

In today's tech space, most products are really a collection of other products bundled together to (hopefully) achieve a design objective. They tend not to work as well as a product that was designed wholly in house; Google Android customers are finding that out today, because Google doesn't make the hardware. You need to own the whole ecosystem to make really good products.

And the same holds true for the rest of the customer experience beyond the intrinsic product. In most of the tech space, manufacturers can't control distribution, can't control the retailer, can't control setup, and can't control service.

Such experiences scream for the need for whole products. Products are better if they are whole on both the inside (the stuff that makes the product work) and the outside (the rest of the customer experience during the ownership and use of the product). Today it seems that most manufacturers work to perfect the "core" product and are satisfied if the tangential elements of the product are nonnegatives; few take the steps to turn these elements into real customer experience positives.

Steve Jobs and Apple didn't see things this way at all. They led the free world—the technology world in particular—in terms of holistic, or whole-product, thinking. They worked to deliver a complete customer experience to fit the visions and customer needs that we've been examining.

Sure, complete products are nice from a design and experience viewpoint. But done right, they can also make money. Since the demise of cameras and film, and disregarding razors and blades as a far simpler product platform, we haven't seen anyone find a way to monetize a customer relationship after the sale the way Apple does.

The holistic product and holistic customer experience become a win-win both for the customer and for Apple. The customer gets a better, more complete, and, at the risk of using an overused word, seamless experience. Apple gets residual revenue after each sale, keeps control of the customer experience, and, especially lately, gets and retains access to huge amounts of customer information (some say too much).

From the Beginning

Steve Jobs had a whole-product, total customer experience orientation from the beginning. He first saw it in the creation of an entire product in a simple, user-friendly cabinet, the Apple II (designed to resemble a consumer-friendly Cuisinart cabinet that he had seen in a department store, as the story goes). The idea grew with the availability and use of VisiCalc (although not developed by Apple) as a solid application for the Apple II.

The whole-product idea really marched into town with the early Macintosh. The Mac was really "turnkey"—ready to use, with no need for configuration or add-ons. Everything was on-board in a cabinet that was simple even by today's standards. The OS was integrated with the product. At the time of the introduction, Steve saw a new laser-printing engine under development at Canon, and immediately hooked up with Canon to develop and market a version—the LaserWriter—especially for the Mac. When Apple doesn't actually develop an accessory or software itself, it works very closely with the vendor to make sure the development is done right, and it tries to sell the product under its own name where it makes sense and where possible.

Holistic design leads to better products. Apple gets to manage the experience. Quality improves; there are fewer "blue-screen" failures. The channel gets more to sell. The customer gets a solution. What more could you want?

Who's Minding the Store?

Under Steve Jobs, Apple continued down the path of integrating the whole experience through the life of the Macintosh. Steve had visualized direct delivery of Macs to consumers from a FedEx hub, assuming control of that part of the process and gaining more customer touch. At the time, Apple had exclusive authorized resellers (dealers) and some presence at large retailers, but no direct channel. The direct-channel idea, however, was nixed by a skeptical John Sculley, who instead looked at distribution as a multitier model and a battle for shelf space—à la the soft-drink industry.

That conflict, among others, led to Steve's departure. But the vision of selling direct to consumers as part of a whole-product platform never went away.

What came next—after Steve's 1996 return, of course—was iTunes in 2001. Based on a software platform purchased from a third party and modified, and a then-novel approach to getting paid for music downloads (which Steve had to work hard to negotiate with the recording industry), the iTunes Store was born. Now, for the first time, a store was really part of Apple's product. The iTunes Store not only allowed for easy and seamless purchase, but also managed a buyer's music library from a distance. And of course, Apple then became a big player in the music industry, with an estimated more than $1 billion in annual iTunes revenue.

The App Store for the iPod and then the iPad followed soon after. The model was the same—to provide a seamless way for customers to shop, buy, and download apps for their devices. Customers can choose from an assortment of free and paid apps in 12 categories, from business and education to games and entertainment. The App Store builds the customer experience and loyalty while also generating substantial revenue. (Apple doesn't break out revenue figures for iTunes or App Store sales.)

The App Store and iTunes added a lot to the postsale customer experience. But what about the presale experience? What about postsale product support?

The first Apple Retail Store hit the ground in 2001, and there are 357 of them as of July 2011. Carefully crafted and staffed, the stores were meant not just to sell products, but to "make deep emotional connections with customers." They were designed in such a way as to carry the simple, elegant, sleek, plain tech design of the products forward into a beautiful and compelling physical space. Trained salespeople walk the floor, and the "Genius Bar" at the back of the store holds up the support end of the experience. By setting up these stores,

Steve Jobs went against the conventional wisdom, despite the failure of Gateway stores and the aborted launch of Dell stores. But the way the stores completed the customer experience was unique and delighted customers; shopping in an Apple Store is a pleasant experience even for those who don't own an Apple product.

Apple Stores, like everything else in the Apple universe, are part of the Apple whole product. The Apple whole-product components are designed to the same standards as the products themselves.

The Apple platform doesn't just *support* the customer experience—it *adds* to the customer experience.

"SIMPLE CAN BE HARDER THAN COMPLEX"

Look at (or, these days, pick up) an Apple product. What are your first impressions? Smooth; substantial; solid; sleek; sexy; simple. I'm running out of "S" words, but no matter. Apple products have an elegant simplicity that is matched by none except a few design-centered Bang & Olufsen audio products dating back to the 1960s. But beyond appealing, attractive design, the elegant simplicity stretches much further.

Simply put, Steve (another "S"; how about that?) sought a level of refinement and sophistication that would run laps around most competitors. It wasn't just about how products looked, it was about how they *felt*. And it wasn't just about how products felt, it was about how they *worked*.

If he had put his mind to the task, Steve would probably have been a pretty good designer himself. But he was better at creating a vision, letting his design specialists do their thing, and then working with the result. In 1992, one of the bright spots in a relatively dull Apple era was the hiring of the industrial designer Jonathan Ive, a Brit who had previously worked for Apple as a consultant. Ive favored a very clean, sleek, high-tech look, with lots of white plastic, aluminum, titanium, and stainless steel; flat surfaces; and minimalist designs for control interfaces, plugs, and so forth. Initially he worked on the original PowerBook laptops and reached his stride with the 1998 introduction of the colorful iMac, an Ive brainchild. He is credited with the design of the iPod and runs something of a monastic design lab at Apple. Today he is the senior VP of industrial design.

In 2008, the *Daily Telegraph* named him the most influential Brit in America.

LESS IS MORE

Simplicity is not just an objective, it's a passion. To Steve, a product was more sophisticated when it was simple. It takes a higher design standard to make something simple. As Steve shared in a 1998 *Business Week* interview shortly after returning to Apple: "Simple can be harder than complex. You have to work hard to get your thinking clean to make it simple. But it's worth it in the end because once you get there, you can move mountains."

Mark Twain once said, "If you want me to give you a two-hour presentation, I am ready today. If you want only a five-minute presentation, it will take me two weeks to prepare." Many others have echoed the same sentiment.

For Steve and his team, the 40-button mobile phone was a nonstarter. Having one button was the design objective, and it took some extra work to get there. The beautiful graphics interface and simple touch controls, brought forward from the iTouch, were the result. Apple wants all of its products to be the "five-minute speech": the one you understand, the one you remember.

Along these same lines, in a 2006 *Newsweek*/MSNBC interview, Steve shared: "Look at the design of a lot of consumer products—they're really complicated surfaces. We tried to make something much more holistic and simple. When you first start off trying to solve a problem, the first solutions you come up with are very complex, and most people stop there. But if you keep going, and live with the problem and peel more layers of the onion off, you can oftentimes arrive at some very elegant and simple solutions. Most people just don't put in the time or energy to get there. We believe that customers are smart and want objects that are well thought through."

Less is more. So I should stop here. You get the point. Do the extra work to make it simple. Made simple; done right.

More Than Mere Products

What Steve Jobs saw in products, he also wanted to see in product families, and in organizations. For Steve, "Simplicity and focus are one and the same."

Consider what happened when Steve returned to Apple and reduced 350 products to 10 products on a simple four-quadrant grid. Do you think this helped the product teams focus? The sales team? The channel and retail stores? The customer? You bet.

Likewise, Apple's organizational structures are simple. Most high-tech firms have people scattered in cities and beautiful mountain towns all over the place. An HP product, for example, might be designed by teams in California, Colorado, Houston, and Massachusetts, each doing a piece of the design. Time zones, voice communications, and even cultural differences add friction to the process. Steve kept his design teams small, simple, and together. The recently announced three-million-square-foot "spaceship" headquarters in Cupertino was designed in part to get all the design teams under one roof—they had been scattered in locations within about a five-mile radius of the current Infinite Loop headquarters.

Product simplicity. Organizational simplicity. *Focus.* It's that simple.

DON'T FORGET THE COOL

Apple products have long been described as cool; in fact, for many admirers, they've become almost synonymous with the word "cool." Steve Jobs was known to use the word quite a bit himself.

But what does the word "cool" really mean? It's fun to look at all the snippets and scraps of slang definitions for the word. Apparently the "hip" form (in contrast to the temperature, the color, or the mood form) of the definition emerged in African American jazz clubs in the 1930s and has meant pretty much the same thing ever since. Here are a few definitions and phrases that connect with our sense of cool:

- Single-word definitions include "fashionable," "accepted," "admired," and "approved." Another somewhat vague definition is "an aesthetic combining attitude, behavior, and style," although this does not say much about what kind of aesthetic.
- A more specific definition is ". . . something with 'Zeitgeist,'" although now we must reach into the

German language for a definition of Zeitgeist—
the "spirit of the times" or "spirit of the age."
Another rather graphic and alliterative definition
is "avoiding mental straitjackets."

Take your pick.

So we still don't have a clear set of criteria; there's no
checklist for "cool." Perhaps it's like pornography or the
innovation culture discussed in Chapter 6: you know it
when you see it. A leader looking for a dose of cool in a
product would look for these things:

- A modern, futuristic look, product, and package
- Fine, simple lines and the finest materials
- Extraordinary sensory qualities—touch, feel, sound
- Simplicity and quality in human interface—solid,
  easy-to-use controls and buttons
- Seductive and sexy; makes you want to look at it,
  touch it, listen to it repeatedly

Whatever cool is, Steve Jobs knew it when he saw
it—and he knew that customers were willing to pay for
it. Steve Jobs invested in products and invested in individuals such as Jonathan Ive to keep things cool.

What Would Steve Jobs Do?

It may seem that much of this applies only to the tech industry. If you're running a company that makes bathroom cleaners or one that operates a taco restaurant, does any of this apply? The truth is that it takes some thought, some practice, some experimentation, and, yes, some tolerance for failure. But even if you're in one of these less sexy businesses, you still have a whole product. If you sell bathroom cleaners, your customer must prep, use, and dispose of the cleaner, and protect her clothing while using it. There are sensory experiences, including the post-cleanup aroma. And maybe you can come up with a cool package or dispenser or holder, so cool that even the teenagers in the family want to try it.

If you're running a taco restaurant, think again about the whole product and the whole experience, from the time customers arrive until they depart. Service, cleanliness, and sensory experience all count and count big. Instead of viewing them as necessary evils, view them as a chance to differentiate your restaurant, to show excellence above and beyond the taste of the food. Keep the menu, the décor, and the service simple. Elegantly simple.

Like In-N-Out Burger, which we visited in
Chapter 4.

The short speech again: think complete, simple,
and cool.

Here are some Jobsian product strategies:

- Always think whole product.

- Look at whole-product components as
  opportunities to excel, not just to meet the
  competition or get the job done.

- Think elegant; think simple.

- Keep the organization simple, too.

- Don't forget cool—sleek, seductive, and sexy.

CHAPTER 8

MESSAGE

And he could sell. Man, he could sell.

—*Walter Mossberg, October 5, 2011*

At the Apple Music Event in October 2001, the first iPod was introduced. Here's a three-minute excerpt from the nine-minute presentation.

The field we decided to do it in—the choice we made—was music. Now why music? Well, we love music. And it's always good to do something you love. More importantly, music is a part of everyone's life.

[slide, in room-sized format, on wall behind Steve: A part of everyone's life (large target market)]

Everyone. Music's been around forever. It will always be around, this is not a speculative market. And because it's a part of everyone's life, it's a very large target market all around the world, it knows no boundaries. But interestingly enough, in this whole new digital music revolution,

[slide: No market leader]

... there is no market leader.

[slide: brand logos of Creative, Sonic/blue, and Sony]

There are small companies like Creative and Sonic/blue, and there's large companies like Sony that haven't had a hit yet. They haven't found the recipe, no one has really found the recipe yet . . . for digital music. And we think, that not only can we find the recipe, but we think the Apple brand is going to be fantastic, because people trust the Apple brand to get their great digital electronics from.

[slide: Portable music]

So let's look at portable music. Let's look at the landscape.

[slide: first reveal—picture of CD player]

The first thing, if you want to listen to music portably, you go out and buy a CD player. Right? That's one way to go. You can play 10–15 songs. *[second reveal: picture of flash player]* Or, you can buy a flash player. You can go out and buy one of those. *[third reveal: picture of MP3 CD player]* You can buy an MP3 CD player. *[fourth reveal: hard disk space player]* Or, you can buy a hard disk space jukebox player. These are the four choices for portable music right now. So let's take a look at each one of those.

[slide with header "Player   Price   Songs $/Song"]

[first reveal: CD $75   15 $5] A CD player costs about $75, holds 10–15 songs on a CD, and costs about five dollars a song. *[second reveal: Flash $150   15 $10]* You can buy a flash player, pay about double that, about $150, and it holds the same 10–15 songs, for about $10 a song. *[third reveal: MP3 CD $150   150 $1]* You can go buy an MP3 CD player, and with an MP3 CD, which you can burn on your computer, costs about $150 but holds 150 songs, so you get down to a dollar a song. *[fourth reveal: Hard drive $300 1000 $0.30]* Or, you can buy a hard drive player for about $300, it holds about a thousand songs and costs about 30 cents a song.

So we looked at this and studied all of these and *[highlighting Hard drive line on slide]* said, "That's where we want to be." That is where we want to be. And we are introducing a product today that takes us exactly there, and that product is called *[slide: iPod]* iPod.

iMac. iBook. iPod.
iMac. iBook. iPod.

The presentation continued for six minutes, defining the iPod and its benefits, and demonstrating how it worked. It wasn't the most dynamic or the most entertaining of Steve's pitches. Most of his pitches, surprisingly to some, had a fairly serious tone. But it was a great example of the style and substance that Steve delivered repeatedly and predictably for years, especially after his 1996 return to Apple. In very simple, straightforward terms, he conveyed the need, the problem, the solution, and how it works. The need, the product, and how to use it. Why, what, and how.

Steve didn't just give the simple, straight, and clear three-step program. He loaded it with market insight, built it up, and brought it to a dramatic and memorable close. After his presentation, you knew exactly what the product was, why it existed, and what it was for. You knew why you came to watch, and you remembered every bit of it.

Some great leaders fail because they're brilliant and accomplished but can't get their message out to others. Others are great at the message but have nothing to say. Steve Jobs was a master at both. A lot of leaders get the nuts and bolts right and guide their organizations to do some pretty good things, but they fail because they can't or won't get the message out. They can't sell. They can't evangelize. They can't *inspire*.

Steve Jobs gave an excellent example of how the message not only sells the product and the company, but also energizes the organization. He was a great example of how getting the message right also establishes and sells you as a leader.

BE THE FACE OF YOUR COMPANY

Steve became not only the public face of his visions and the public face of his products, but also the public face of his company.

What could be simpler? And yet, do we see other business leaders on stage, or in any other format, doing this? We touched on this in the previous chapter. When was the last time you saw a corporate leader in the same video frame as one of his products? Let alone explaining the market, explaining the product, and explaining how it works?

Lee Iacocca set this standard at Chrysler. We've seen Dave Thomas evangelize hamburgers for Wendy's. We've seen Herb Kelleher giving us down-home talks from the center aisle of one of his Boeing 737s. We've seen a few snippets of Sam Walton and Bill Coors here and there. But for the most part, American CEOs and business leaders have stayed away from the product, stayed away from the stage, and stayed away from the company's message. They've let the ad agencies take over.

Of course, that's part of what made Steve's spokesmanship so unique. It wasn't only that he did it, but that he did it so well. We looked forward to his annual January Macworld appearances because we would find out the next really cool thing that was coming from Apple. We were also energized because billionaire Steve Jobs took the time and made the effort to talk to us. He talked to us at our level, as though he were sitting in our living rooms demonstrating the product. It made us respect him and his company all the more. It *inspired* us.

And, as we'll discuss in a minute, it also inspired his employees. Wouldn't you work enthusiastically on a product that your CEO made a huge personal effort to promote? Yes, of course you would. It would give you as an employee validation and a sense of pride in what you do. What you do is important. What you do means something. What you do is worthwhile.

It's hard to put a finger on why other CEOs and business leaders don't take advantage of such a huge opportunity. A CEO or leader who is willing to "eat his own cookin'" will bring popular appeal to the product and to herself. Such a willingness builds credibility and makes the relationship between the customer and the company more human. If nothing else, it saves money, as expensive actors and other substitutes don't need to be brought in.

Personally conveying the message shows passion. It shows commitment. It shows that you're behind the product, the culture, the vision, and the customer.

In the case of Steve Jobs, the message became part of the whole product.

Outside In

How do you deliver a vision? How do you deliver a major strategy speech that defines your path to the world—in eight short minutes? How do you announce in five minutes a product that will change the world? Steve Jobs was a master at understanding customers, creating visions, building an innovation culture, and delivering products.

But there was *one more thing*: Steve Jobs could sell. He could evangelize. He was also a master at delivering the message about the customer, the vision, and the product. By the time the presentation was finished, you knew exactly why the product was made, who it was for, what customer problem it solved, and how it worked. Steve's amazingly simple message sold the product to customers, to channel partners, to platform partners and software developers, to the trade press, and to venture capitalists and financiers on the outside. But that's not all. Steve's presentations went a long way toward selling and evangelizing the vision and the business to the *inside*—to Apple employees.

I believe that from the start, Steve's messages were crafted to serve two masters—to evangelize outward and to evangelize inward to build and reinforce the culture. Steve's talks inspired employees to be creative and productive, and they reinforced the vision.

It was an immensely positive cycle. Deliver the vision that inspires your team to produce great products that you evangelize to the world—which in turn inspires your team onward. What other CEO, or business leader at any level, do you know of who does this?

THE MESSAGE—SIMPLE AND ELEGANT

Like everything else in Steve Jobs's world, his messages were handcrafted to perfection and were hallmarked by a simplicity and an essence of good design.

First, he would set the stage. His opening statement was often something like, "Every once in a while, a revolutionary product comes along that changes everything. . . ."

From that point on, most of Steve's presentations followed a fairly common structure:

- *Why we need it.* As part of setting the theme in the opener, Steve would describe the current situation, why it leaves something to be desired, and what Apple wants to do about it. If there were any numbers or tables in Steve's slides, this is where they would enter the discussion. The tables and figures usually described a current market. Frequently there was some accompanying history—early products and their impact, the history of PC evolution, and the like. However it was assembled, this part of the pitch set the stage.

- *What it is.* Once the stage was set, Steve would introduce the product, typically with a dramatic buildup exemplified by the repeated "An iPod. A phone. And an Internet communicator" that lined the audience up for the iPhone. There was usually a graphic showing the product, and, depending on the size of the product, one was usually available in his shirt or jeans pocket for him to show.

- *How it works.* Up to this point, with the right preparation and stagecraft, any CEO or business leader who was so inclined could probably do these steps. Lay out the market; describe a product. Most of them would have to work on the style and flair for drama that Steve brought to the event, but it's not too far away from the sorts of presentations made in corporate conference rooms all around the world—except that it was externally, not internally, focused. But what really set Steve apart—and this became the third element of his message—was a typically fairly detailed explanation—really, a show—of how the product actually works. Steve gave a demo of the product as if he were sitting with you one-on-one in your living room. This part was truly unique, for it showed Steve's level of involvement in and commitment to the product—and your experience with it.

Once we had sat through, and typically enjoyed, this demo, there was usually some kind of enticing or leading close. Steve would tell us how the world will change. And then there was the famous, "And there's one more thing," where some really cool product feature, like the new graphics interface for OS X, was rolled out. These "one more things" created anticipation and excitement that even most ad agencies cannot dream of.

These three elements came through whether Steve was announcing a new product to the world or a new business plan to a sitting board or venture capitalist. It's little wonder that Steve's expert corporate communications coach, Carmine Gallo, called him the "world's greatest corporate storyteller."

THE POWER OF THREES

Speaking of the "three elements," Steve liked to keep things simple, and he had a way of doing so by grouping ideas and concepts into threes. We just saw it with the iPod/phone/Internet connection device buildup.

Markets were divided into thirds; presentations were divided into thirds; the evolution to the iPod (iMac, iBook, iPod) was divided into thirds. Besides Steve's penchant for simplicity, there were other reasons to do this. Researchers have found that people can digest only three to seven things at a time, so if you have a presentation slide with nine points on it, don't bother. In the tech world, simplicity is king, and in Steve's world, simplicity was king, so he opted to keep it closer to three (and fewer if he could).

I've done this in my *"The 100 Best Stocks You Can Buy"* series of investment analysis books, too. I give three pros and three cons for a particular investment. Not only does this keep the analysis in focus for the customer, but it goes a long way toward keeping you in focus, too, as you analyze or try to understand something complex.

Try it. You'll like it. It works.

SPECIAL DELIVERY

Steve Jobs's presentations were enviably simple, engaging, informative, exciting, comfortable, and fun.

His delivery style was almost as important as the content itself. Steve set the theme, told you what problems were being solved, set a road map for the solution, created memorable moments, and left the audience wanting more.

Few others, if any, in the corporate world, have come close.

Although carefully rehearsed—for hours, according to most accounts—his presentations were casual in nature. From the moment he walked on stage in his trademark black turtleneck, jeans, and white shoes, the people in the audience were put at ease, figuring that they would be addressed by a favorite artist rather than a hard-charging executive. It worked.

The presentations were choreographed and rehearsed down to the finest details. Images were few, but they were shown in full-room size behind Steve. Most were dazzling versions of Apple's simple logo, magnified and colorful images of an Apple product, or very simple tables or lists of facts or bullets. Clean, concise, and colorful.

Steve had an oral style that is difficult to describe and best learned by watching it (a list of some favored presentations on YouTube appears at the end of the chapter). He was calm and confident. He was clear and articulate, using short sentences and simple words, very seldom "techie." There were almost no "ums" or "ahs" or filler words. The cadence and flow were almost ideal, with pauses and silence in the right places to allow the audience to digest his message or to build excitement. He was genuine and credible; it was pretty clear that he was saying what he thought, not what the audience wanted to hear.

The presentation, the accompanying visuals, and the message were crisp, visually simple, and easy to grasp.

All of these traits and manners are plainly visible in the videos, and I believe they can be learned or developed with the right amount of focus and rehearsal. Beyond this core, there were a few other notable trademarks of Jobs's presentations.

No Corporate Speak

How tired we all get of hearing about paradigm shifts and scenarios and eyeballs and leading edges. How tired we all are of hearing words like "basically" and "going live" and "deploying" and "fast track." The language of business is saturated with buzzwords and jargon that, at day's end, mean little. There's actually a game about it. You can play "Bullshit Bingo" at a business presentation by sitting with a customized card listing these expressions. The first to line 'em up wins (see www.bullshitbingo.net; try it, it's fun). Anyway, the point here is not to amuse but to highlight Steve's clear rejection of the typical "corporate speak" style.

Steve used simple, insightful, and fun words and phrases, such as, "It's gorgeous," "It's amazing," "They don't get it." Main Street words, not headquarters words or techie words.

Always the Showman

There is no question that Steve had a flair for the dramatic. He knew how to present a product almost like a three-act play or a gripping novel. The facts that lead to the chase. The chase. And how it all happened and what we get out of it.

He was a master of expression, of pregnant pauses, and of inflection. He knew just the right moment to pull a product out of his shirt pocket. From one image to the next, and from one statement to the next, the audience was hooked and waited for the next big thing to come from the show. There was always a dramatic, applause-capturing close. Of course, Steve used this idea to its full advantage with the "and one more thing" after-announcements.

...But Unpretentious

Good showpeople typically tend to take over, to overpower, and to be more about themselves than about the subject at hand. Steve carefully avoided this. The casual attire started this off right, just right. We could all imagine being Steve up there, presenting our latest product. The focus wasn't on the man or the image, but on the subject and the images of the subject. Not once did you hear of his own personal successes, and rarely anything of his own stories. In fact, you seldom heard "I."

Not For Laughs

You would think such a gifted and younger-than-most icon presenting his youthful products to an often-youthful shorts-and-sandals Silicon Valley culture would be given to humor, jokes, innuendos, and twists on words.

Not so much Steve.

Steve was a pretty serious guy. He stayed to the point and to the message, and if he threw a little humor at you, you remembered it. But unlike so many speakers, it was clear that Steve didn't need to use humor to keep your attention, and he knew it.

Famously, when introducing OS X in 2000, he told us that the "buttons on the screen looked so good that you want to lick them." He might also use humor to poke fun at a competitor (usually Microsoft): "Our friends up north spend over five billion dollars on research and development, and all they seem to do is copy Google and Apple."

He used humor not to entertain, but rather to make a point, and make it clearly. In this way he was a bit like, but more subtle than, other exceptional leaders such as Abraham Lincoln, Winston Churchill, and Warren Buffett.

STEVE JOBS ON STAGE

If you do a search for "Steve Jobs" on YouTube, you'll come up with about 27,100 entries. Naturally, not all of these are unique speeches; there are multiple entries for many of them. But even so, there are dozens of unique presentations out there for you to take a look at. Here are a few of my favorites (you can search the first few words of each of these titles on YouTube to find them):

- Macworld San Francisco 2000: the Mac OS X introduction, 9 minutes, major software product introduction and demo
- Steve Jobs introduces the "Digital Hub" strategy at Macworld 2001, 8 minutes, major product vision and strategy
- October 2001 Apple Music Event: the first ever iPod introduction, 9 minutes, strategy and new product platform
- Steve Jobs's 2005 Stanford commencement address, 14 minutes, June 2005
- Introducing the new iPhone, Part I, 10 minutes, January 2007
- January 2010 Apple iPad: Steve Jobs keynote, Part I, 6 minutes, introduced the iPad and its benefits

Grab an Odwalla, turn on your iPad, and learn to spread the perfect message.

WHAT WOULD STEVE JOBS DO?

As we've seen, Steve Jobs didn't stop at creating the product and the customer experience. No way. He evangelized the product and its supporting vision to such an extent that it almost became an extension of the product. Both the content and the style were unique as compared to most corporate-style speeches, and he used the message in ways most people don't think about. Here are a few pointers:

- *Never forget about the message.* It can be just as important as the product.

- *Be your product; be your brand; be your company.* Don't miss this opportunity. Don't leave it to the PR people. People inside and outside the organization really respond.

- *Don't forget: your presentations in public mean a lot to your team inside the four walls.* It's a golden opportunity.

- *Keep your content simple and in groups of three.* "Why we need it, what it is, and how it works" is a good starting point for organizing a message.

- *Keep the language simple.*

- *Remember, you're on stage; use the opportunity.* But avoid making yourself the center of attention. It's about your product and your message, not about you.

- *Be confident, be current, and have fun.*

CHAPTER 9

BRAND

I have some very bad news to share with all of you. Steve passed away earlier today.

—Apple CEO Tim Cook,
October 5, 2011

Steve. Just Steve. Just like Mike.

We all know who Mike is. But few other people in history have succeeded in making their *first* name their brand. And even fewer—maybe no one—in the history of business have done so. What would Steve Jobs do? What would Steve do? What other Steve *could* we be talking about?

In the days immediately following Steve's passing, the media, the talk, and the chatter on the street were just about Steve. Everybody knew the story. Like Mike, he touched millions of lives, whether you're a basketball fan or not. Because of Mike, many of us *became* basketball fans.

But basketball doesn't touch our lives the way personal technology has come to touch our lives. Steve was a respected and revered role model in an industry that touches us every day, and an industry that touches us more than ever and in a more positive way than ever because of what he did. And in an industry that is little known for producing the kind of folk hero Steve has come to be.

People compare Steve Jobs to Thomas Edison and Henry Ford. Thomas Edison and Henry Ford also created products—really, industries—that touch our lives every day. They also contributed great things to the business philosophy and ethos of the day, a day when the philosophy and ethos of business were in none too great shape.

But did they have the personal charisma of Steve Jobs? The customer-centered vision? The sense of elegant, simple personal design? Could they deliver a keynote speech or introduce a product the way Steve Jobs did? The lack of widespread media and technology may have hampered their efforts. But even if they had today's media at their disposal, it's doubtful that either of the two would have moved the needle with the charisma, the passion, the personal charm, the clarity, and the empathy that Steve Jobs exuded on a daily basis.

Thomas Edison was an innovative technologist. Henry Ford was an innovative business leader. But neither became a brand. Steve Jobs became a brand.

BRAND ESSENCE

We can talk for hours about how to build a product brand. And many people have done so; the literature and Internet resources on this topic are extensive. So I won't go into the details, but the character traits of product or company branding boil down to a few basic themes:

- *Image.* The company or product gets a recognizable label, jingle, and/or tagline. The image creates recognition, is easy to see and to remember, and may convey a thought, a physical characteristic, or a promise. Tide and McDonald's create recognizable

orange and golden arches images, respectively,
which over time have come to mean something
bigger to the consumer about the product and the
company.

- *Consistency.* A brand connotes consistency, especially in today's world of national brands. Eat at a
  McDonald's anywhere in the world, and you will
  get pretty much the same Big Mac. Buy a box of
  Tide anywhere in the world, and you'll end up with
  clean clothes.

- *Promise.* The image and consistency evolve into an
  intrinsic promise of a certain quality, a certain level
  of value, a certain taste, a certain style, and a certain
  level of comfort. Four Seasons has a more luxuri-
  ous brand promise than Holiday Inn has.

- *Trust.* The promise, successfully delivered time and
  time again, creates trust. The higher the degree of
  trust, the more valuable the brand.

There's no doubt that the value of a good brand is
huge, and in today's world of short product life cycles
and reduced attention span, the value of a good brand is
greater than ever. People trust good brands and are willing to pay more to get them. The value of the Starbucks
brand to that company is almost incalculable, and was
from the beginning. The value of the Apple brand has
become just as incalculable.

The kind of branding that fewer people talk about, and what I think Steve's leadership legacy is really about, is establishing a *personal* brand—a personal brand as a leader. A personal brand incorporates the traits of a product brand, but goes way, way beyond them. Mike may have done it in the basketball world; Tiger did it in the golf world (until his own behavior destroyed the promise and the trust). But nobody in the business or technology world has ever done it better than Steve.

ON DEVELOPING
A PERSONAL BRAND

As a starting point, a personal brand includes all the elements of a product or company brand—*image, consistency, promise,* and *trust.* Those traits can be developed in a person, too, and a person, especially a leader, with those traits will succeed. But people have personalities, attitudes, and behaviors that no product can have, and that companies can have only as a sum total of all the parts.

With products and companies, trust is key; if people don't trust the product or the company, about the only thing a marketer can do to move product (besides repairing trust) is to cut prices. With people, it's about trust too, but it goes a bit beyond just being able to depend on them. People create things; they decide things; they express emotions about things—there's more to it than just whether the product works or is a good value. With people, the "trust" thing evolves into *credibility*.

Several traits contribute to the kind of credibility that Steve possessed and shared every day:

- *Respect.* As an individual or a leader, you gain respect by being right, by admitting when you're wrong, and—this is what most leaders forget—by respecting others.
- *Optimism.* A person who is optimistic looks forward and is willing to move forward, and is less likely to be bound by the norms of the past. This person dwells in the future, not in the past.
- *Passion.* Mix optimism with perseverance and spend every waking hour thinking about it and evangelizing it, and you'll win the hearts of your followers.
- *Confidence.* A confident and self-assured leader makes others around him more confident.
- *Altruism.* Good leaders think about others and try to put themselves in their place. They want everyone to succeed, not just themselves.
- *Professional style.* Good leaders develop a consistent work and communication style that everyone knows and learns how to work with. As we saw with Steve, it doesn't have to be an easy style, but it has to inspire confidence. When a leader is difficult

to work with or keeps others off balance, those
people tend to focus on their relationship with the
leader, not on the product or the project. When
people know you're a game changer, it means that
they can be game changers too.

• *Personal style.* Everything from your clothing and
attire to your desire for privacy to how you present
yourself inside and outside the organization defines
your personal style. Steve's casual clothing told
everyone that he was an artist; he was genuine and
"one of the people," not a "dress to impress" type.
Steve's focus was on the product and the customer,
not on himself, and everything about him—what
he wore and what he did at Apple and at home—
suggested this.

Steve built himself into a unique business and technology brand. That brand represented consistent innovation, a consistent desire to change the game in the
customer's favor, and a consistent application of the
complex secrets of technology to better our personal
lives. Steve also stood for consistent product excellence,
consistent customer experience excellence, and consistent design excellence.

Steve's brand was almost as much about what he
wasn't as about what he was. He wasn't about money. He
wasn't about the corporation. He wasn't about politics.

He wasn't about executive image or grandeur. He wasn't about owning lots of companies, and he wasn't about owning many fancy houses or jets or owning a car collection. He wasn't about being the center of attention. He wasn't about power.

He kept the focus on the message and not on himself. Steve mostly put people at ease, giving them constant assurances that the product and the customer were the important things. He was just a regular guy to work with as the situation required, with no pretense and no formalities. Sure, he could be difficult if things weren't going right, but that was part of the brand, too.

Clarity was an important part of his brand and his style; even the words he chose, from "insanely great" to "that's shit," are legendary. The elegant simplicity of his own style fed his products, and vice versa.

PERSONAL BRAND MATTERS

Steve set such a high bar that many doubt if anyone will ever be so successful at establishing a personal brand. There are other game changers out there, like Sergey Brin and Larry Page of Google and Mark Zuckerman of Facebook. But none of them have the style or charisma or respect or influence that Steve enjoyed, and, while people can and do grow, they don't appear to be moving in that direction.

The "Steve" brand is all the more amazing when you consider the business he was involved in. The fact that Steve built his brand and maintained it so consistently for 35 years in the face of changes in technology and tastes is all the more remarkable. Many people think the changes that led to his departure and his return in 1997 went a long way toward affirming his brand—he was "right after all." Without that test—and without the chance to achieve excellence with *Toy Story* in a field that he knew little about going in—perhaps nobody would have noticed.

Steve made and led people to huge accomplishments, and he enjoyed a life arc that simply isn't available to most of us mortals. He established a huge personal brand, lived up to it, and lived off it, and that brand success will forever remain hard to duplicate. But that doesn't mean you shouldn't try to build your own personal leadership brand.

Why is a personal brand so important? Especially for a leader?

When you establish an excellent personal brand as a leader, your followers know what to expect. They get the idea. They get the theme. They get it. And they trust it. Your personal brand is recognizable and consistent, and it conveys a message. It serves as an example. It is developed and cultivated through experience, combined with a certain sense, a certain style, and a certain image.

People will assume you're right, not wrong. They will align with your vision. They will look at what they can do for you and your company, not for what you and your company can do for them. They will trust that under your direction, their work won't go to waste, that it will lead to great things, and that they will be appreciated for it. All of this moves the needle from apathy to motivation to inspiration. Never has a business leader inspired so many people so completely as Steve Jobs.

PERSONAL BRAND, COMPANY BRAND

Those of you who are following the six-step Steve Jobs Leadership Model offered in Chapter 3 may have come into this chapter expecting a quasi-academic treatment of building consumer and company brands. Nope, that's not what's here. Sure, Steve, and Apple, built a tremendously valuable consumer brand, a brand to be envied and emulated. No arguments on that.

If your only success as a leader is to develop a brand with the value of the Apple brand, you'll be a huge hit, even if nobody recognizes your name and none of your employees know who you are. The corporate landscape is littered with successful brands that were built and are supported by nameless faces in corner offices in thousands of corporations. Who, without looking, could name the CEO of Procter & Gamble or McDonald's or Walmart off the top of their heads?

And yet, these leaders are successful by most measures of corporate success—just look at the track record and continuing growth of their organizations. They may have effective personal brands inside their organizations. Or they may carry out the necessities of executive leadership just well enough to keep their organizations going. Or they may have just the right subordinates in the right places to get things done. Or they may be just plain lucky.

When you contrast these generic leadership styles with the more branded leadership styles of Howard Schultz of Starbucks and Larry Ellison of Oracle—and Steve Jobs at Apple—however, it becomes apparent that by developing your own personal brand, you can clearly move the needle on the company's brand. The company's brand develops your personal brand, and vice versa.

Now, most of you reading *What Would Steve Jobs Do?* aren't CEOs and aren't planning to become CEOs anytime soon. But the same traits that drove Steve's success can drive yours, no matter what organization you're in, and no matter what your role in that organization is. Whether you run your own business, manage call center telemarketers, or are an individual contributor and project manager with no direct reports in a big firm, these principles all apply.

Build your personal brand, and people will follow you anywhere.

REACHING THE SUMMIT

So how do you build your own personal brand? How do you reach the elusive last step, the last stage, of the Steve Jobs Leadership Model?

Easy. You excel at the first five steps, evangelize them to your team, and develop your trademark style:

- *Customer.* Focus externally. Learn everything you can about the customer. *Be* the customer. Be the customer's advocate. Consistently ask, "What does this do for the customer?" Develop a visible passion for the customer.
- *Vision.* Try to see over the horizon. Develop a vision, test it, communicate it inside and out, and be willing to adapt it to reality.
- *Culture.* Create a can-do environment, one that rewards, not hampers, creativity. Make sure the process within your team supports new ideas and customer-focused visions.
- *Product.* Focus on the product. Get involved in the details, know it inside and out, and make sure it's what customers want.

- *Message.* Be the spokesperson for your product and for the team. Evangelize. Go inside and outside. Attend trade shows; be your own media rep; build your brand in your industry, not just your company.

Then there's the style thing. This is a bit less linear. The idea is to develop a personal and professional style that is consistent with the vision. If your vision is to get customers to be more creative and think differently, then black mock turtlenecks and jeans are probably more effective than thousand-dollar business suits. You should convey an image that you think your team will like, and that you think your customers would like if they met you in person.

WHAT WOULD STEVE JOBS DO?

Again, building a personal brand isn't linear; it's not a precise template. If it were, everyone could and would become Steve Jobs! It is something that you'll have to visualize, dream about, experiment with, and modify:

- *Focus on the five supporting steps* from the leadership model: Customer, Vision, Culture, Product, and Message.

- *Keep them in balance.* Don't be all about message or all about product or all about vision. It won't work.

- *Be passionate.*

- *Don't overdo it.* Let your actions speak for you. People recognize when you're trying too hard.

- *Be driven by achievement, not power.*

- *Be driven by achievement, not money.*

THE LEGACY LIVES ON

The "Think Different" ad copy, first aired in 1997, the year of Steve's return to Apple, says as much about Steve's personal brand as I can. It makes a fitting ending:

Here's to the crazy ones.

The misfits.

The rebels.

The troublemakers.

The round pegs in the square holes.

The ones who see things differently.

They're not fond of rules, and they have no respect for the status quo.

You can quote them, disagree with them,
glorify or vilify them.

About the only thing you can't do is ignore them,
because they change things,
they push the human race forward.

And while some may see them as the crazy ones,
we see genius.

Because the people who are crazy enough to think
they can change the world are the ones who do.

INDEX

ABOUT THE
AUTHOR

Peter Sander is an author, researcher, and consultant in the fields of business, personal finance, and location reference. He has written or collaborated on 27 books, including *The 100 Best Technology Stocks You Can Buy 2012, The Innovation Playbook, The Dentsu Way, Value Investing for Dummies, The 100 Best Stocks You Can Buy 2012, 101 Things Every American Should Know About Economics*, and the Cities Ranked & Rated series. He is also the author of numerous articles and columns on investment strategies. He worked for 21 years as a marketing program manager for a major Silicon Valley tech firm and has an MBA from Indiana University. He lives in Granite Bay, CA.

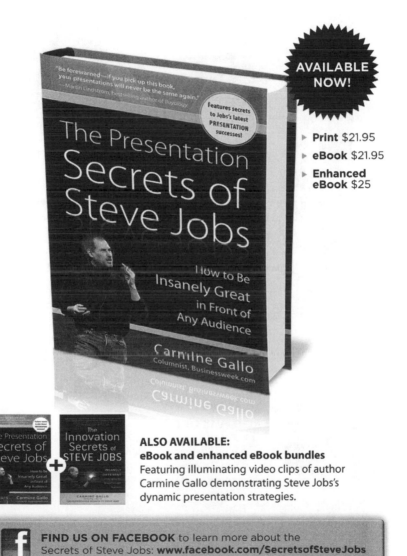

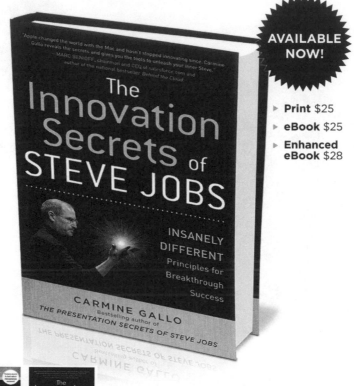